Becoming Me

Finding my true self in God

Becoming Me

Published by JMB Books, Sydney NSW

© Jo-Anne Berthelsen 2016
www.jo-anneberthelsen.com

Cover by Kim Hall
Layout by Book Whispers www.bookwhispers.com.au

National Library of Australia Cataloguing-in-Publication entry

Author:	Berthelsen, Jo-Anne
Title:	Becoming Me: Finding my true self in God / Jo-Anne Berthelsen
ISBN:	978-0-9946443-0-5 (pbk)
Subjects:	Berthelsen, Jo-Anne
	Self-discovery
	Spiritual growth
Dewey Number:	248.4

All rights reserved. No part of this publication may be reproduced, stored in, or introduced into a retrieval system, or transmitted, in any form, or by any means (electronic, mechanical, photocopying, recording or otherwise) without the prior written permission of the publisher.

Unless otherwise stated, all Scripture quotations are taken from the HOLY BIBLE, NEW INTERNATIONAL VERSION, Copyright © 1973, 1978, 1984 International Bible Society. Used by permission of Zondervan Bible Publishers.

Scripture quotations from THE MESSAGE. Copyright © by Eugene H. Peterson 1993, 1994, 1995, 1996, 2000, 2001, 2002. Used by permission of NavPress. All rights reserved. Represented by Tyndale House Publishers, Inc.

Scripture quotations are taken from the Holy Bible, New Living Translation, copyright ©1996, 2004, 2007, 2013, 2015 by Tyndale House Foundation. Used by permission of Tyndale House Publishers, Inc., Carol Stream, Illinois 60188. All rights reserved.

Becoming Me

Finding my true self in God

JO-ANNE BERTHELSEN

Jo-Anne has penned a heartfelt, honest and deeply searching self-reflection, beautifully and sensitively written. I'm sure it would lead any reader into a personal inner journey of their own. It is also a proclamation of God's love and faithfulness which will inspire and encourage spiritual reflection for all who enter into *Becoming Me*.

Dr Carol Preston, counsellor and author of *Beyond the Fight, Next of Kin* and eight other historical novels

Becoming Me has all the qualities we look for in autobiography—honesty, insight, relevance and eloquence. We all have life stories that have inherent value, but not many of us possess the levels of self-awareness and honesty Jo-Anne Berthelsen displays in her latest offering. She draws out an abundance of perceptive insights from her experience. At each stage of her story she pauses to open up reflective questions for us to consider our own lives in the light of her observations. These are especially relevant for anyone considering questions of identity and vocation. And this is all conveyed in the assured writing style of a masterful storyteller.

Dr Rick Lewis, mentor to Christian leaders via Anamcara Consulting, author of *Mentoring Matters*

In *Becoming Me*, Jo-Anne recounts the dealings of her soul with her Creator and Saviour from her birth to the present day. It is a privilege to read how she has committed her walk through life to the Lord and how he has directed her path. Her story illustrates the fact that we do not find our identity in our talents, gifts, efforts or inclinations, but in Christ alone.

Marion Andrews, author of *My China Mystery*

At one level, Jo-Anne Berthelsen's *Becoming Me* is a very personal account of her own discovery of her 'true self'. But at a deeper level, it is a gentle invitation to journey with her, to find our own, deepest, truest self, that is, who we are in the eyes of our loving, Father God.

(Rev) Ray Evans, teacher, counsellor, chaplain

In *Becoming Me*, Jo-Anne shares honestly, showing us that she has walked the walk regarding dealing with her personal issues. With Jo-Anne at your side, you too can go on a journey of discovery, using her questions at the end of each chapter to reflect on your life. I would recommend this book to anyone who wants to reach their full potential as a person.

Sue Banks, counsellor, Crisis Support Coordinator Lifeline Sydney & Sutherland

I am awed by Jo-Anne's raw honesty, vulnerability and determination. Many themes run through her courageous story. One is finding her place in a Christian world dominated by traditional values. Her poignant struggle with her worth and deep longing to live with integrity will move you.

Paula Davis, trauma counselling specialist, marriage and counselling educator, adjunct lecturer

Becoming Me is a book to be read prayerfully, allowing God the opportunity to extend His healing hand as we progress. A truly honest story which takes us through the innocence of childhood to the maturity of our middle years. It describes how our early experiences leave their mark on the core of the person we become, but also how the power of God's grace and love can deliver healing into the poverty of our souls. A gentle yet challenging read.

Susanne Timpani, author of *Twice Stolen* and blog '10 Minute Daily Retreat'

Contents

Acknowledgements   xi
Introduction   xiii

Chapter One
    Seeking Self-Worth   1
Chapter Two
    Seeds of Achievement   13
Chapter Three
    Fears and Fallacies   26
Chapter Four
    A Passionate Purpose   39
Chapter Five
    Changing Goalposts   53
Chapter Six
    Inspired by Love   70
Chapter Seven
    Challenged to Step Out   86
Chapter Eight
    Learning and Growing   100
Chapter Nine
    Called to Serve   115
Chapter Ten
    Delving Deeper   128
Chapter Eleven
    Letting That Creativity Loose   141
Chapter Twelve
    Staying Real   155
Chapter Thirteen
    Coming Home   169

For my beautiful grandchildren, Amy, Olivia, Zain and Maxine, with love. May you each rejoice in your God-given uniqueness, rest in God's amazing love and realise your full potential in life, as God guides and sustains you.

Acknowledgements

To my manuscript readers/editors Lorene Noble, Jane Louise and Marion Andrews, thank you so much for your helpful suggestions and meticulous, time-consuming work on my behalf.

To Rochelle Manners, thank you for your honest advice, generosity of spirit and excellent, ongoing support in my publishing journey.

To Kim Hall, thank you for your gentle, servant heart and for using your wonderful creativity to bring a book cover I love into being.

To those who wrote endorsements, thank you all for your gracious words and taking on this task, in the midst of your busy lives.

To my email prayer team, both past and present—Joy, Joan, Ruth A, Ruth S, Kerry, Marjan, Rhondda, Michelle, Judy, Patricia, Anne—who have tracked with me through so many speaking engagements and writing projects, thank you from the bottom of my heart.

Introduction

I have always had a fascination for those sets of matryoshka dolls—or babushka dolls, as they are often called—those little, wooden Russian families nesting inside one another and decorated with bright, intricate designs. I love to see all the effort that has gone into creating the colourful, hand-painted versions and admire the vivid imagination of the artists responsible for each one.

When I first began to consider writing this book, the image of some Russian dolls I own came to mind at once. I remember well how I could not resist buying them some years ago—I had wanted a set for so long. I was visiting London for the first time and found my five little purple painted people at a market stall near the church of St Martin-in-the-Fields in Trafalgar Square. They were part of the magic of that moment and I treasure them to this day. For me, they typify the sense I have had in more recent years that my own outer layers are peeling off and I am at last discovering that most intrinsic part of me—the kernel, if you like, of who I am and who I was created to be.

For some of you, your true identity may have become clear to you quite early on in life, by God's grace. But for others, that journey may have been much longer, with many twists and turns, as has mine. Some of you may have had your dreams and aspirations derailed for years or perhaps even your whole life by illness or the need to care for others or lack of funds or some other life situation. Yet, whatever challenges we may face, we do not have to let them prevent us from growing within ourselves and with God.

In the following pages, I share my personal experience of finding my true self in God, in order to encourage all of you to undertake or continue on your own journey of discovery. But I write in particular for those who may have found that journey a little daunting or discouraging. As you read, may you know you have not been forgotten or cast aside. Just as God sought out Adam and Eve when they hid in the garden in the cool of the day, as Genesis 3 describes, so God keeps on seeking us out all through our lives, calling our names, longing to connect with us on a deeper level.

Now is the time to be honest with God and with yourself, leave those hiding places within and allow God to help you discover more of the person you were created to be.

You are made in the image of God, created to reflect something of who God is to the world.

You are unique.

You are known.

You are valued.

You are loved.

Chapter One
Seeking Self-Worth

For you created my inmost being; you knit me together in my mother's womb. I praise you because I am fearfully and wonderfully made; your works are wonderful, I know that full well. Psalm 139:13-14

'So ... who is Jo-Anne?'

I gazed in surprise at the person seated opposite me at our friend's birthday party. Her chin was cupped in her hand as she stared at me with bright, enquiring eyes across that dinner table, waiting for a response. I already knew her, although we had not seen each other for some time. We had even chatted earlier in the evening and caught up with each other's news. So why was she asking me such a question? Was she joking?

At that point, I remembered she had worked as a counsellor for many years and was also involved in mentoring several women. Perhaps she truly was seeking to know what makes me tick, who I am at the core of my being, what drives me to do what I do and to write the books I write.

I smiled and began to answer her with a passion that seemed to surprise her.

'Well, I know I'm God's much-loved child—that's who I am, first and foremost. And I know that in creating me, God has given me unique ways to bless the world. So I'm also a writer and speaker. That's who I feel I am at the core of my being. I love reaching out to others via the written and spoken word and touching hearts with God's love—it's so satisfying and fulfilling. It's not that I believe any of my previous roles or occupations were a mistake. I can see how each of them equipped me to do what I'm doing now, which I think is what God created and gifted me to do.'

The reason I had a ready response for her was that I had thought long and hard about such questions in the course of my writing journey in particular. Yet for many years—in fact, until well into my forties—I would have had little idea how to answer my friend's query. Prior to that, I was too busy being the person my family, my friends and even my church wanted me to be—or the person I *thought* they wanted me to be. I had very little self-worth. Instead, I was a total people-pleaser, full of self-doubt and so concerned, above all else, about what people thought of me.

That evening at the birthday party, I watched as my friend went on to ask others a similar question. Some appeared to answer with even more alacrity and enthusiasm than I had. Perhaps they were among the fortunate ones, I decided, whose concept of who they are has always been clear to them so that they have never doubted their worth or their unique, God-given gifts. Yet I also noticed several who looked uncomfortable when confronted with such a forthright question and seemed to struggle to know how to respond. Perhaps, like me, they had grown up uncertain of their value or their place in this world. Perhaps they had even experienced that same vague yet profound feeling I had so often experienced about myself that they were, in fact, some sort of mistake.

My earliest memories seem permeated with a sense of being inadequate in some way and a disappointment to my parents. Why this was the case is mere conjecture because, at the same time, I knew I was loved and wanted. My sister was almost three years old when I was born in 1948. I was given the name Jo-Anne in honour of my maternal grandmother, May Josephine. At some point in my growing up years, I remember being told what the nursing sister at the hospital in Brisbane where I was born had said, on hearing what I was to be called:

'Oh, Jo—she should have been a boy! She'll always be a tomboy and come home from school dirty and untidy.'

Did her comment stem from the fact that Jo could also be a boy's name? Or was this nurse perhaps thinking of the tomboy character Jo, the second eldest of the four March girls in Louisa May Alcott's literary classic, *Little Women*, so popular at the time? Whatever the case, my mother often maintained this nurse was prophetic, whenever I came home during my early school years with shoes off and the sash of my dress undone. I also remember many occasions when my father would tease me in a resigned tone about my untidy appearance or about some rough and tumble action of mine. He did not mean to be unkind, but I always resented his comments and would react accordingly.

'Jo—she should have been a boy! Jo—she should have been a boy!' he would chant, with a wry smile and a twinkle in his eye.

Some years later, I discovered my parents had had a stillborn son around three years before my sister was born. We were told he died in the womb six months into the pregnancy—a traumatic event for my parents and one from which my mother took a long time to recover. Nevertheless, she found the courage to try again and my sister was the result. When I arrived three years later, however, it was decided there would be no more children after me. I suspect this decision was made on the basis of my mother's physical and emotional health, although finance could also have been a factor. Or perhaps the plain truth was that they were quite content with the two daughters they had. Yet as I grew up, I began to wonder whether my father was disappointed he did not have a son. Was he only joking when he said I should have been a boy? Would I always be second best in his eyes? I wanted so much to be reassured I was special to him, despite being a girl. I wanted to know I was of as much worth to him as any son.

I knew he loved me, although he did not always seem to know how to show this, to my satisfaction at least. And I loved him. As a young child, I often chose to be with him when he worked in the yard or when he went on some errand or another. It made me feel important and wanted. On one occasion when I was about three or four, I had gone somewhere with him in an old truck he owned that had no cabin doors—and, of course, no seatbelts in those days. As we turned at a busy intersection not far from where we lived, I stood up, excited because we were almost home. Before my father could do anything to save me, I slid out of the cabin and landed on the road with a thump, right in front of a much larger truck. The shocked driver managed to stop just in time, then jumped out, swearing loudly and shaking like a leaf. He scooped me up in his arms and ran with me to a nearby shop where, unbeknown to him, my mother's cousin happened to work. To this day, I can still remember her holding me close and comforting me. I was fine—but I remember sensing how upset my father was and suspect he took much longer to get over this event than I did. He loved me dearly and would have hated anything to happen to me.

I also recall another occasion when I was with him in our own backyard. He was a keen gardener and I decided I would help him out with all his jobs in our vegetable patch. I gathered up my skirt and formed it into a pouch, as I edged along the neat rows of tomato bushes he had planted. The tomatoes were quite large at that point and a nice, shiny green. I picked so many that they became too heavy to carry, so I made my way over to where he was working.

'Look, Daddy! Look at all the tomatoes I've picked for you!' I showed him with satisfaction.

I can still hear the roar that emanated from him and how I scattered those green tomatoes in all directions, as I ran as fast as I could up our steep backyard. But I was not fast enough. My father was close behind, smacking those plump, little legs of mine all the way until I reached our back steps and the safety of my mother's arms.

'Don't smack her! She didn't mean it—she didn't know it was wrong!' my mother cried out, holding me close and trying to defend me.

In later years, I realised why he had been so angry. That vegetable garden and that lovely crop of tomatoes in particular were his pride and joy. But back then, I did not understand at all—and I was devastated. I had so much wanted his praise. Instead, I had managed to incur his wrath.

Yet Dad also had a much softer side which he tried to show in his own bumbling way. Many times in the late afternoon, as he relaxed in the lounge before dinner with the evening newspaper, I would crawl into his lap and curl up against him. With a resigned sigh, he would endeavour to hold his newspaper open and keep reading, all the while with a squirming child on his lap. The time came, however, when he refused to have me sit there anymore.

'No, I can't have you on my knee. You're too big now—you're too heavy,' he said one day with finality.

In my heart, I knew it was true, but I still remember how hurtful those words were. I wanted to feel of worth to him. I wanted him to be happy to have me snuggle up close. Instead, this rejection, as small and unintentional as it was, left me feeling fat and babyish and embarrassed.

Although our family was not what would have generally been classed as well off, we did not lack any of the essentials. My father was a hard worker, sometimes taking on other jobs besides his regular one as foreman in a milk factory. As well, he always kept himself busy with various handyman tasks or minor building projects around our home. These included a new sun deck above our garage on one occasion and an extensive patio and barbecue area on another. We lived in an old, weatherboard house on 'stilts', with ample space underneath for my father's carpentry workshop, as well as for his boat and fishing tackle. But gardening was his forte and our lawns and garden beds were always immaculate.

Our house was always immaculate on the inside too. My mother prided herself on her housekeeping abilities and was an excellent cook. She was a fulltime housewife and cared for us well—perhaps too well at times. She worked hard, but also tended to worry a great deal about all she did and about everything else, it seemed to me, which I suspect impacted me more than I realised. As a young child, I am told I was often to be found with my thumb in my mouth, looking out at the world with some apprehension in my big, brown eyes. And I was always more than willing for my sister to take charge and lead the way in whatever venture we were undertaking. Even at this early stage of my life, there was much uncertainty and self-doubt within me and little concept of my worth as a child of God.

I do not remember feeling any apprehension about starting school the week I turned six, however. I had wanted this day to come for so long and knew my sister would look after me. I loved school from the outset. I enjoyed learning new things and conquering whatever academic challenge the teacher gave us. Yet I often felt different—as if I did not quite fit in. I was tall for my age and quite solid, a fact that did nothing to boost my self-esteem. I was not built for speed and did not enjoy running or playing any sort of game that required good coordination. I seemed to have been born clumsy, often tripping over and skinning my knees or falling off my bike or dropping things or tearing my clothes. I had thick, straight, brown hair, which was cut quite short by the time I started school. And from the age of seven, I wore glasses—big, round ones that qualified me well for that taunting title of 'Four Eyes', so popular at the time. I believed I was unattractive and felt that, however hard I tried, I would never be popular or accepted by the 'in' crowd. To my shame, I remember how I reacted one afternoon on my way home from school when some boys began to tease me.

'Ha-ha! Four eyes! Four eyes! Look at her! Such a goody-goody, teacher's pet.'

'Yeah—hey, you don't even swear, do you? Bet you don't!'

'Yes I do!'

'No you don't!'

'Yes I do!'

'Well, show us then!'

'Okay, I will! You're a ... and a ... too! You don't even know what the ... ... you're talking about.'

I remember feeling so disappointed in myself even as that string of expletives left my mouth. But I was desperate to show those boys I was not the boring, goody-two-shoes they thought I was. Whatever the cost, I wanted that peer approval that would make me feel worthwhile and accepted.

I also longed to wear the latest clothes or fashion accessories, just as the popular girls at school did. But our family could not afford such things and I doubt our mother would have thought them appropriate anyway. I wanted to be able to go to the pictures each Saturday afternoon, as many of my classmates did, to have more pocket money, to buy more lollies. Instead, I learnt the piano, sang in a choir and followed other equally serious and worthwhile pursuits. At times, I even tried to make myself sound a little less intelligent and a little less concerned about whether or not I had done my homework, in order not to stand out from my classmates. Some years, I talked a lot in class. I suspect I was often bored, but I also wanted to be accepted, to make others laugh, to draw attention to myself. I tried out for various sports teams and athletics events when I was quite aware I was not good enough. I entered art competitions when I was hopeless at art—all for the sake of being popular and having others see me as someone interesting and exciting.

I grew up, then, with a marked lack of self-worth, despite always doing well at school and despite excelling at piano and singing. I was not pretty enough. I was too proper. I was too bright. I was too big. I was too serious. I was just ... well, just too much of an all-round good girl. Yet I did not want to be viewed as less than good either. From an early age, I hated being disciplined by my parents in any way. It was bad enough merely to be told I was naughty, let alone to be smacked for something I had said or done. My pride was too great and my self-esteem too fragile to be able to handle any criticism well or to receive even the slightest rebuke.

'I'm *not* a naughty girl!' I would maintain, sobbing and heartbroken.

Yet, for some reason, I still insisted on pushing the boundaries at times. To my shame, I suspect I became quite wilful and arrogant as I grew older. As a result, my parents resorted to keeping a special stick handy in our kitchen to be used on me with force whenever I overstepped the mark. At one stage, they had to reach for it so often that I christened it 'Jo's Smacking Stick', writing these words on it in bold letters with a mixture of resentment and plain cheekiness. I did not react well to being judged to be in the wrong, whether the accusations were just or not. I was always quick to defend myself, always wanting to clear my name as soon as possible. The alternative of taking the blame on board was unthinkable.

I could not bear anyone outside our family to view me in a bad light either. A few times during my primary school years, I remember being taken to task by a teacher in front of the whole class for talking too much or some other slight misdemeanour. On each occasion, I was sure I would never recover from the humiliation of it all. After I read L M Montgomery's *Anne of Green Gables* in Year Three, I found I could relate with ease to Anne Shirley's feelings that day in the Avonlea schoolhouse when Gilbert Blythe teases her and she is punished for retaliating. I too suffered from wounded pride on these occasions and mulled over what had been said to me for days after. I wanted everyone to like me and yearned for acceptance from teachers and peers alike.

Yet, on the whole, I know I had a happy childhood. I was loved. I was well cared for. I had my sister to play with and to forge the way ahead for me. There were extended family members who also loved me—in particular, my maternal grandparents. As well, I always had one or two good friends at school. And I was given every opportunity to develop my musical ability and pursue other interests. Nevertheless,

I was convinced deep down in my heart that I was somehow worthless and flawed—big-time.

As far as my religious understanding was concerned, I was aware God was an important Being to be honoured and treated with great awe and respect. And I knew basic facts about Jesus from an early age, including the fact that he died for me. I am sure we sang 'Jesus loves me, this I know' and other similar songs with great gusto at the three different Sunday schools to which my sister and I were sent during the course of our primary school years. No doubt I was also taught I was made in God's image and likeness, as Genesis 1 tells us, and that everything God created was good. At times too, I would have heard Psalm 139 read aloud in church, including the beautiful words of verses 13 and 14:

For you created my inmost being; you knit me together in my mother's womb. I praise you because I am fearfully and wonderfully made; your works are wonderful, I know that full well.

Yet it was years before I would come to grasp the fact that God had fashioned me—yes me, that little girl Jo-Anne—in my mother's womb with such care and was delighted with the end result. And it took much longer still for me to comprehend that God had made me as I was for a purpose—that I had been created in God's image and likeness to do the things only I could do. I began to internalise these truths more in my mid-teens, when God broke into my life in a new and unforgettable way, although it was not until I was almost forty that I felt their full impact. As a child, however, and on into my early teens, I did not have that comforting knowledge of God's love and that strong sense of security that comes as a result of such a loving relationship. Instead, I looked to my own abilities and achievements and, in turn, to the opinions of others, to validate me as a person. I did not realise I could allow God to shape my self-worth in a way I could not refute, to whisper deep and profound words of encouragement into my spirit, assuring me I had value and significance.

I am unsure why such realisations did not dawn on me earlier than they did. Perhaps it had to do, in part at least, with the natural process of growing up and learning to be my own person. At one stage as an adult, I undertook a type of recovery course that included a session entitled 'The Shame Game' and later went on to conduct this same course myself at our own church. As I taught that particular session, I found myself strongly relating to the points I made and so easily able to explain how we manage our sense of shame by hiding from God and others. Even as I did, it dawned on me that this was what I was still doing. But no, it could not be, I told myself—I was too old and too mature in my faith to continue harbouring such childish concepts. Anyway, I could not own up in public to such things. After all, I was the group leader. I had to keep up appearances.

So the nagging sense that I was flawed and inadequate and the constant need to cover up who I was at the core of my being remained. Although I was loath to admit it, I began to realise that the deep sense of shame Adam and Eve experienced when the Lord God desired to meet with them in the garden, as recorded in Genesis 3, was also in me. In their case, they felt ashamed because of their disobedience, so decided to hide themselves. And I too knew I had fallen short of God's standards in so many ways. Yet it went deeper than that as well. It was not so much what I had done in my life but who I perceived I was as a person that caused my all-pervading sense of shame. Much better to hide and reveal to the world only that part of me that might be regarded as good enough or interesting enough or clever enough.

How many of us, down through the centuries since that first man and woman, have bought into this same lie that we are worthless and unacceptable, both to God and to others? I have come across more than a few in our years of ministry—mature adults in other aspects of their lives—who still struggle with a significant lack of self-worth and who cannot fathom why God made them the way they are. For some reason or another, the realisation that they are created in God's image and, as such, have at least one unique and wonderful aspect of God within them to share with our world has eluded them.

I understand and relate to this struggle. If it were not for God's intervention in my life in a variety of ways over the years, I could still be in that position myself. Even now, if I am not careful to stay close to God, I can stumble in this area. Even now, on those occasions when I choose to listen to that harsh, accusing voice of the enemy rather than the loving, affirming voice of God, I can find myself wallowing in those old feelings of worthlessness and self-doubt and wanting to run away and hide. Yet, each time, God reaches out to me, rescues me and brings me home once again to that place where I know I am so loved, so accepted and so secure.

For reflection

- Look at your hands. Think about the fact that each of us has a unique set of fingerprints—even identical twins. Then consider how God has created human beings with such care and intricacy out of billions of cells, each of us with our own unique DNA and our own unique retinas in our eyes. Next, read Psalm 139—out loud, if possible. What is God saying to you about yourself through all this?

- In Jeremiah 1:4-5, we read:

    The word of the Lord came to me, saying, "Before I formed you in the womb I knew you, before you were born I set you apart; I appointed you as a prophet to the nations."

    Reflect on this as far as your own life is concerned and jot down your thoughts.

- Many years ago, there was a poster around containing the words: 'God don't make no junk!' Apparently, this was a statement often made by Ethel Waters, a singer with the Billy Graham organisation and herself the result of her mother's rape. What is your response to these words?

- Create a piece of artwork using your own name or write your name in several ways, using different styles and colours. As you do this, note how you are feeling. When you are finished, try putting this creative experience into words.

Chapter Two
Seeds of Achievement

Yet when I surveyed all that my hands had done and what I had toiled to achieve, everything was meaningless, a chasing after the wind; nothing was gained under the sun. Ecclesiastes 2:11

Pride goes before destruction, a haughty spirit before a fall.
Proverbs 16:18

We are all different. And we all respond in different ways to life's challenges and opportunities. While I enjoyed a happy, secure and perhaps rather sheltered childhood, others may have endured many painful, difficult times when they needed to be strong to survive. While some are blessed with many wise family members and friends around them to help and guide, others may be forced to muddle through life themselves as best they can. While some may have always felt accepted for who they are and affirmed for doing their best, irrespective of the outcome, others may have experienced overt or covert pressure to try harder, to be the best, to seek to achieve in everything.

During my high school teaching days, I saw many students with little sense of self-worth give up almost before they started, at least in the subjects I taught. Some could not be encouraged to try at all, however much help I offered them. They had covered themselves with various protective layers—defiance, disengagement, even quiet despair—and their attitudes showed they were certain they would fail, whether they bothered to make an effort or not. Later, during our ministry years in an area where there were many marginalised people, this sense of hopelessness was almost palpable. It could often be seen in the faces of those who came to our church for food and other forms of emergency relief and heard in the things they said. For far too many, it had become a stifling, soul-destroying force from which they tried at times to escape via alcohol or drugs or some other unhealthy, destructive means that served only to make life worse for them.

But there are those with low self-worth who choose a quite different route in life. Their drive towards perfectionism is strong and they strive to prove themselves in every part of their lives so that others will have to take notice of them. Perhaps they will even become popular in the process and succeed in attracting a large number of friends and followers. Yet the happiness and fulfilment they would like to find so often remains out of their grasp. So the vicious cycle kicks in, over and over again, each time bringing even more self-condemnation. As Hurley and Dobson state:

> [Achievers] *resent themselves for not measuring up to their own standards. Judging themselves inadequate, they are prone to depression and lack of self-esteem.*[1]

This was the road I chose, as if drawn along it by some huge, invisible magnet. As I grew up, I came to believe with all my heart in the crucial nature of success and achievement in proving my worth to myself and others. Perhaps this belief began to flourish even before I started school when my sister would often take great delight in treating me as her pretend 'class', in order to practise her teaching skills on me. But I did not mind—I was keen to learn. And that did not change after I set off with her to primary school.

Once there, I discovered I had no trouble coping with whatever

---

1   Kathleen V Hurley and Theodore E Dobson What's My Type? HarperCollins 1991 p 20

work I was given. At that time, our school year was divided into three terms, with exams at the end of each of these. During my first year, I managed to come top of my class in all three terms, to my great satisfaction. From then on, I formed the unshakeable belief that this was something I had to continue to do at all costs. As soon as I saw how pleased and proud my parents were with my results, I became determined never to disappoint them in any future exam.

On several occasions in the years that followed, I remember walking home from school, holding my precious term report card in my hand and thinking how terrible it would be if I had to tell my parents I had failed to come first. I could not bear the thought of it. Yet I knew my parents were truly proud of my sister's results, even when she came anywhere other than first. She too always did well in her exams, despite fierce competition from several other excellent students in her class. I was aware that coming anywhere in the top few in a class such as hers was quite an achievement—but, for me in my own class where I had far less competition, it was first or nothing. At that time in Queensland, children spent eight years at primary school, which meant that, all up, I sat for twenty-four term exams during those years. I tried my best and ended up coming first in all twenty-four. Once, early on, I tied for first place—and that to me felt almost like failure.

I had set the bar high indeed. But I knew I had to keep up such a standard of achievement because this was what made me feel special and worthwhile.

Somewhere during those years, I discovered neither of my parents had ever attended secondary school. My father was born in Coolgardie in the goldfields area of Western Australia. For a time at least, his father worked on the railways, which may well have meant that my father and his four brothers found it difficult to get to school on a regular basis. The family soon moved to Perth, but again, education did not seem to have been a high priority. Why this was the case and also what my father's childhood dreams might have been remain a mystery.

In our teens, my sister discovered Dad could not read at all well, a fact we suspect prevented him from undertaking anything other than the factory work he did throughout our growing up years.

My mother's childhood in country Queensland was quite different. Education was important in Mum's family, especially since my grandfather had been a teacher himself at one stage. Despite that, during her later primary school years at least, it seems Mum was kept home from school at times to help her mother with the washing and other household tasks. While some of my mother's four sisters and two brothers did finish high school and pursue further studies, with two becoming teachers and one a nurse, Mum chose instead to work in the local post office after leaving school. She was an intelligent woman, I believe. Yet, for some reason, she decided further study was not for her.

It is understandable then that both our parents were proud of all our school achievements and enjoyed our success in a vicarious way. Perhaps it even added to their sense of self-worth, just as it did to mine.

I became then the clever, serious-minded, 'Four Eyes' girl who was always top of the class and hence not much fun to be around, at least as far as many of the other students were concerned. I loved reading. I loved writing stories and compositions. I loved spelling and analysis and parsing. I loved practising handwriting in our special school copybooks, using a long, fine-nibbed pen and ink from the inkwells in our desks. I loved tracing maps with great care from my atlas and learning about other countries. I hated Maths, but persevered and somehow did well in it, at least in those early years. And I managed to have a good relationship with most of my teachers. Towards the end of primary school, I would be excused from class at times in order to do jobs such as taking notes from the principal to the teachers, checking school supplies in the stock room and making the teachers' morning tea. In my final state-wide Scholarship exam, an important milestone which often dictated which type of secondary education we could undertake, I achieved 93.5%, one of the top ten highest results gained by students in state primary schools that year.

My parents were, of course, delighted—my mother could almost not contain herself. Some years earlier, a teacher who had taught both my sister and me at different stages had informed her that, in her opinion, my sister was the better student. That did not worry me at all, but it seemed to have irked my mother. The day the Scholarship results were made public via the morning newspaper, as was the custom then, she made a point of phoning this teacher.

'Good morning, Miss Denniston. How are you? ... Yes, I'm well, thanks. ... Did you see in the paper that the Scholarship results came out today? ... Well, I just wanted to make sure you knew Jo-Anne scored 93.5%! ... Thank you. It's a higher mark than her sister's, so she did better after all ...'

I felt deep embarrassment as I listened to her boast about me. Even then, I remember wondering how anyone could compare results obtained in exams held in different years. I suspect my mother could not bear to see either of her children criticised and was determined to do her best to stick up for me. But it became clear, as my sister and I later progressed through high school, that we had quite different gifts and abilities. My sister would often end up helping me with subjects such as Maths, Chemistry and Physics in which I floundered, rescuing me time and time again when I did not understand something. Yet, despite realising how different we were, I still felt an inward pressure to prove myself equal to her in whatever way I could. That need to achieve planted in my mind so early on continued to grow in my life, on both a conscious and subconscious level.

Both of us were given every opportunity to succeed in extra-curricular activities such as music, elocution and sport, as well as at school. While my father's wage might not have been high, my mother, always the one to look after the finances, took care to ensure there was enough put aside for such interests. I was nine years old when I began learning piano. I loved it, but, as I reached the stage of sitting for exams, that familiar drive to achieve kicked in. Even now, as I remember those years, I squirm, just as I did on those hard chairs in draughty corridors outside music rooms when I waited, heart in mouth, for my turn to come with the examiner. I swallow, trying to get rid of that sour taste in my mouth as I recall what an effort it took back then not to rush outside and throw up somewhere. In my mind, I hear the student before me stumble while playing a scale and stop. An awkward pause follows. I wonder if I will do the same and feel shame at even the thought of it. My stomach feels so tense—my teacher has urged me to play without music, but will I remember those pieces I have practised so often? My turn arrives. Nothing can save me now. All I can do is try my best.

All these memories come flooding back in an instant. I remember too the agony of waiting until my music teacher received those exam results. In my child's mind, it seemed like an eternity. Each afternoon as I walked home from school, I would wonder if she had phoned my mother to give her the news. Would my teacher be disappointed in me? Even more to the point, would my parents be disappointed in me? I hoped and prayed I had managed to reach that magic honours mark of eight-five or more. Anything less would have been a failure, from my perspective. And I was sure my parents and teacher felt the same.

My father seemed to want me to succeed as a singer as well. When I was around eleven, my parents took me to audition for a new junior choir at the Conservatorium of Music. Again, I felt so nervous and insignificant as I was ushered into the director's studio and stood there alone, gazing at his rather craggy, intimidating face and shock of white hair. He surveyed me over his glasses as he sat at that beautiful grand piano, then pointed to a spot on some sheet music in front of him.

'Now, Jo-Anne, please sing these notes for me.'

I stumbled my way through it, stopping once to correct myself, but he seemed satisfied.

'Hmm—good. Now ... I'm going to play Middle C, then another note after it. Can you tell me what that second note might be?'

I hummed the first note he had played and continued humming my way up the scale under my breath, trying to count the number of intervals between the two notes. There were four, I decided. Or was it five? I checked again, humming each note aloud this time. Yes, definitely five. That second note he had played must be A then.

'I think it's A,' I whispered.

'Excellent—you have perfect pitch,' I heard him say, to my vast relief.

When my father discovered I had been accepted, he insisted on buying me a new outfit. I am unsure whether he or my mother chose it, but I can remember how wonderful I felt in that blue and white spotted, three-tiered skirt that was all the fashion at that time and my white blouse with the wide sailor collar edged in red. I was delighted to be in this new choir, but just as delighted I had made my father so proud. Later, I joined a different choir which would often give concerts and travel interstate to compete in eisteddfods. Again, my parents supported me by driving me to our many practices and paying for my trips and the special uniforms we were required to wear. My successes and achievements were theirs as well—and I was proud to make them so happy.

My mother always encouraged my sister and me to be committed to any activity or group we were part of and never to let anyone down, whether teachers or leaders or other team members.

'If a thing's worth doing, it's worth doing well,' she would scold, whenever we tried to find some excuse for not turning up at a lesson or not practising for some event or not giving of our best at all times.

I believe part of the reason she taught us this arose from a fear of what others might say about us if we did let them down in some way. But I suspect her father also instilled this attitude in her as a child herself. Our grandfather was a kind but strict and upright man who had achieved a great deal in his own life and inspired us to do our best as well. This wholehearted commitment was evident in my sister's keen involvement in Girl Guides, a movement that fosters the development of leadership, loyalty, patriotism, survival skills and enjoyment of the outdoors. I joined Brownies, the group for younger girls, and later followed my sister into Guides, although with somewhat less enthusiasm. My sister was much more of a natural, outgoing leader, whereas I preferred the safety of following others. Before long, she had obtained badges for proficiency in a wide variety of skills, managing in the end to reach the highest level of Queen's Guide. Meanwhile, I was content to try for badges I knew I could earn easily such as minstrel, musician, singer and entertainer. That way, I would not court failure and my still fragile self-esteem would remain intact.

At high school, I was determined to succeed in every subject I undertook. Yet, in a weird way, it was also a relief to realise I was not the best in my year in all things academic, as I had been for so long at primary school. Now I had to accept I was a little frog in a much bigger puddle where others were quite able to outshine me, particularly in Science and Maths. But I was still proud enough to hate the idea of a teacher thinking less of me for any reason. At one stage, our class had a double Maths lesson on a Monday morning. All the way across town to school, I would go over and over the theorem we had been asked to learn for weekend homework, so afraid my strict Maths teacher, who had also taught my sister, would discover my deep lack of basic mathematical understanding. I can well remember how tense I felt all through the Scripture class that preceded Maths, hoping and praying I could still recall every line of that theorem I had to reproduce as soon as the bell rang.

During her high school years, my sister achieved excellent academic results, not only in Maths but across the board. She also excelled at debating, something I could never envisage myself attempting. On top of that, the year I began at the same school, she was elected girls' Vice-Captain, no mean feat in itself. I was genuinely proud of her. But her success also spurred me on to aim high in everything, for my own sake and that of my parents. I could not disappoint my family—or myself.

Of course, exams were a time of great stress all round. In later years, whenever I happened to open my old Latin books, a strange, musty smell would waft up, bringing with it a rush of memories. Then I would notice the imprints my sweaty, gloved hands had left on the pages, as I crammed those vocabulary lists into my brain during the long tram rides home from school on sticky, summer afternoons. Every moment counted, as I endeavoured to excel. To this day, whenever I catch sight of jacaranda trees covered in their beautiful, purple blossoms, I feel nervous, since this was a clear and ominous sign each November in Brisbane that those all-important, final exams were imminent.

The thought of actual failure in any subject filled me with dread. Yet, on two occasions in my high school years, I came close to doing just that in Physics and Maths. My poor mark in Physics was my own fault, but Maths was a different story. Having endured a succession of mediocre teachers one year, I was one of only two students who passed, out of a class of forty-two students, with each of us scoring a mere fifty percent. It was clear there were reasons for our poor marks besides our lack of Maths ability, but I still hated taking such results home to my parents. Yet, somehow, my name continued to appear each year in that list of prize winners at our School Speech Night. I can remember holding my breath when the time approached for this special list to be announced yet again, wondering if my marks had been high enough to qualify me for a prize, and trying to think what I would do if they had not.

The year after I left school, I managed to fail an exam for the first time. It was an important one—the performance exam for my A Mus A diploma in piano. Disappointed, I decided to try a second time that same year—and failed yet again. The first time I failed, I knew in my heart I did not deserve to pass. I had been too busy with my university studies and had not practised enough. That was all there was to it. But this second failure was a bitter blow to my self-esteem, especially since I missed out on passing by the merest of margins. I also felt sorry to have disappointed my parents, who had poured their hard-earned money into all those piano lessons over the years. Yet I soon came to see what a salutary lesson it was for me. I had often judged other students for their poor results, yet now I had joined their ranks. From that point on, I became much more sympathetic towards those in similar situations.

This experience did not dull my desire to achieve, however. If anything, it strengthened it—my self-worth could not stand any similar blow. I threw myself into my studies over the remainder of my time at university and managed to complete my degree, although it was touch and go with one or two subjects. This, I thought, would be the end of my tertiary studies. However, when an opportunity arose in my middle thirties to return to university, I grasped it with both hands. I did not expect the impossible. After all, it had been a long time since I had attempted any formal study. Yet, deep down, I found I was still that incorrigible achiever, always wanting to impress, always wanting to prove I could do it all, hating the very thought of failure in any shape or form.

Several years later, in my mid-forties, I ended up returning to study once more. And again, I was to discover how well those seeds of achievement planted early on in my life and fed by my previous return to study had continued to grow and flourish. In the end, it was to take the master hand of God to uproot them and to change my whole way of thinking and acting in this area of my life.

Throughout my growing up years and beyond, I believe God was watching over me, protecting me as I tried to impress others with all my achievements and boost my sense of self-worth. I am also sure God reached out to me many times, in an effort to show me how to live and function differently. But I was deaf and blind to such things and wanted to do everything my own way. I did not realise God was quite able, with the most amazing grace, to lift my self-imposed burden of perfectionism from me and quell my never-ending desire to succeed. Instead, I had an entirely different view of God. I believed that, if I did not do well in everything, God would not be pleased with me. This even included, in my early years, knowing all the right answers at Sunday School and confirmation classes. In that part of my life where I should have felt such acceptance, I believed God was frowning at me, waiting to see if I would measure up. I was so slow to learn that, while I might impress others with my high marks and right answers and feel better about myself in the process, none of that made any difference to my standing with God. Instead, God loved me for who I was, not for what I achieved.

In his helpful book *Freedom from the Performance Trap*, David Seamands describes my thinking in this whole area so well. I had swallowed what he calls '*the ultimate lie*':

This lie insists that everything depends on how well we perform—
our salvation and status—our relationship with God
our sense of self-worth—our relationship with ourselves
our sense of security and belongingness—our relationship with others
our sense of achievement and success—our relationship with society around us.[2]

I needed that lie to be broken in my heart and mind in a big way and to experience what Seamands goes on to call God's '*gut-level grace*'—that grace that impacts not only our minds but also the very depths of our hearts.

I am so thankful God never gave up on me and enabled me to experience this grace in later years, along with a sense of much greater freedom in my life. Yet I am also thankful for those years when I learnt to try my best at everything, despite the destructive performance orientation that resulted. Without that drive to achieve, I might never have attempted all the things God had for me to do—and still does. I often marvel at how certain destructive attitudes and experiences in our lives through which the enemy seeks to harm us can be redeemed and transformed under God's hand. I have seen how God can use them to strengthen us and make us more determined, as well as give us

---

2   David Seamands *Freedom from the Performance Trap* Victor Books 1988 p 13

insights into how we can help others in similar situations.

For me, the freedom I enjoy now as a result of God's grace and God's full acceptance of me does not mean I sit back and do nothing. If we love God with all our heart, surely we will want to become all God purposes us to be and seek to use our God-given gifts to enrich the lives of others. We do need to aim high and work hard, giving of our best. After all, Paul's words in Colossians 3:23-24 are still relevant today:

Whatever you do, work at it with all your heart, as working for the Lord, not for men, since you know that you will receive an inheritance from the Lord as a reward. It is the Lord Christ you are serving.

The difference for me now is that, while I work hard and try to achieve good results in all I do, it is not about proving myself to God or to the world at large. It is not about personal glory or making me feel good about myself. Rather, it is about bringing honour and glory to God. It is also about resting in God in the process, knowing I am accepted, irrespective of what successes or failures I might experience in this world. And that is something I need to remember even now, as I write and speak and as I continue to discover how God wants me to live out my remaining years on this earth.

For reflection

- Can you identify any factors in your own background that have caused you to feel driven to over-achieve? What were these and how have you managed to address them?

- Perhaps under-achieving rather than over-achieving better describes your experience. If so, what lies behind this and how has it played out in your life?

- In 2 Timothy 2:15, Paul writes to Timothy: '*Do your best to present yourself to God as one approved, a workman who does not need to be ashamed and who correctly handles the word of truth.*' How would you try to do this as you live and work for the Lord, without allowing yourself to become too focussed on performing or achieving as an end it itself?

- Paul's words in 1 Corinthians 1:18-31 concerning the wisdom of this world and how God has chosen *'the foolish things of the world to shame the wise'* provide some good food for thought in regard to academic achievement. Take time to read this passage aloud and meditate on what God might be saying to you through it.

Chapter Three
Fears and Fallacies

Do not let your hearts be troubled. Trust in God; trust also in me.
John 14:1

Sometimes there seems to be no obvious reason for arriving at the opinions we form about ourselves in our early years or our attitudes to the world around us. Sometimes they seem innate, part of our personality from before we were born. Yet, just as often, as we reflect on the family dynamics around us in our childhood, we can see clearly why we think and react the way we do in certain situations. I am sure my strong desire to achieve stemmed from family influences in my early years—and perhaps this was the case with the fear and anxiety I so often seemed to feel as well. Whatever attempts those close to us might make to hide their own negative attitudes and emotions, somehow our child's inner radar seems programmed to pick them up. How easy it is as children to take these on board and allow them to form yet another layer covering that vulnerable little one hiding deep inside us! And how easy it can be to let such things continue to shape us in our adult years, hindering us from becoming the people we were created to be!

On the surface, I had little to worry about when growing up. My parents loved and cared for me well. We lived in our own home and my father worked hard at his job, just as he did in everything he undertook. My sister was always a strong support, despite our normal sibling squabbles and differing personalities. Yet this family stability did not allay the fears and anxieties I often experienced, including those linked with my need to achieve. What if I did not come first in my class? What if I messed up those scales or that piece of music in my piano exam? What if I did not succeed in the choir audition or gain a role in the school musical? What if my name did not end up on that prize winners' list? I quaked at the thought of such disasters.

At times, I also experienced fears and anxieties on a relational level. I wanted so much to be popular during my earlier years at school when, in reality, there was little likelihood of this. But I still tried—and I feared being rejected in any way. I hated it when those party invitations were handed out and I was not included. I dreaded being talked about or laughed at. I resented the fact that I was not good at sport so would never be able to take that strategic path to popularity. I wanted to be allowed to wear a pretty outfit to school—perhaps a skirt that swung out when I twirled around, just as the girls everyone admired did. Instead, I had to stick to my plain old school uniform of grey pinafore, blue blouse, grey socks and boring, black, lace-up shoes. I wanted to be up with the latest gossip about this or that film star or pop singer, yet no one in my family, least of all I myself, saw enough movies or read enough magazines to know anything about such things.

As I grew up, I came to believe we were quite different from other families in our street. Not many other children lived near us, but I somehow concluded my sister and I were a little above any who did. Early on in my primary school years, I was allowed to play with one special friend who lived nearby on Monday afternoons, sometimes at her place and sometimes at mine. While I might have misjudged the situation, I felt my parents approved of this friend because both her parents were doctors and my aunt, a nurse, worked for one of them. I remember how, one afternoon, another girl whose migrant father ran a corner store near my friend's home asked if she could come to my house as well to play with the two of us. Unwilling to hurt her, I agreed. Yet I strongly suspected my mother would not be impressed.

I was right. My mother could do nothing about it, once the three of us turned up together. But later, we had a conversation I can still recall.

'You mustn't invite anyone extra like that to come and play, without asking me beforehand. Do you understand?'

'Why?'

'Because ... well, because then there are too many of you here together all at once. And you were quite noisy.'

'But she really wanted to come and I didn't want her to be sad. And we had a good time.'

'Yes, but I didn't even know if her parents knew where she was.'

'She asked her dad in the shop and he said yes. I told you that.'

'He might well have, but he doesn't know us and we don't know him. Just don't invite her again—okay?'

I felt embarrassed I had acted in a way that was somehow not right. My mother had made a good point—what I had done was unwise and could have ended badly. But I also wondered even at that age if her response had something to do with the fact that this girl was different from us and therefore not quite acceptable. My parents' attitude in this whole area was more to do with fear of the unknown than anything else, I believe now—they were unsure how to respond to people of different nationalities and backgrounds and felt inadequate even to try. But, whatever their intentions, I used their attitude to bolster my own sense of self-worth and view myself as superior to certain other children.

For as long as I can remember, my mother had suffered from a degree of anxiety—perhaps as a result of her terrible experience of having a stillborn child prior to my sister's birth and her resulting breakdown. Even if it had been more common for women to seek paid employment outside the home when I was growing up, my mother would in all likelihood have not had the confidence to do so. Besides, looking after home and family was a fulltime job for her. Mum expended much energy on keeping the house perfect and the washing and ironing up-to-date. On top of that, baking was her forte—to the extent that she seldom welcomed us into her domain to try our hand at any sort of cooking. She did not drive and did not venture out of the house often, except to shop nearby and to attend family events or church or the Masonic Lodge where she was a member. She was quite a skilled pianist but was too nervous to perform much in public, as was the case with singing, even though I remember her bravely taking lessons at one stage. And, during our teenage years, I suspect she was also a little agoraphobic. On one occasion after we had travelled into the city by tram, she panicked, which resulted in my sister having to accompany her home in a taxi while I took care of the shopping.

My mother's fears and anxieties did not centre on herself alone, however. She seemed to worry about everything in general—and my sister and me in particular. In many ways, she was merely a product of her times in being so concerned about us. She had, after all, experienced the hardships of the depression and war years and wanted us to have the best start in life she could give us. But Mum's worry was extensive and all-consuming. To me, she often seemed overly concerned about how well we did at school and in our other activities, how we looked, whether our behaviour reflected well on our family and whether those who mattered regarded us in a positive light.

'But what would people *think*?' she would often ask us, whenever we wanted to do or wear something a little different from the norm.

This was a big issue for her. She could not bear the thought that we might be laughed at or considered inferior in any way. And she herself, I suspect, was too sensitive and even perhaps too fragile at times to be able to handle any sort of embarrassment we might cause her to suffer.

Later on in my growing up years, whenever I wanted to attempt something that, from her perspective, was too risky and thus fraught with the possibility of failure, she would ask me a different question.

'Oh ... but do you think you can do it?'

This question, put to me in a tone that exuded doubt and fear, often made me more determined than ever to do what I wanted to do. Yet it also undermined my confidence in a subtle way. On the outside, I would appear nonchalant and full of bravado. But inside, the seed of doubt my mother's words had planted would take root, adding to my own self-questioning and anxieties. I am sure her sincere desire was to protect me from falling flat on my face in whatever endeavour I planned to undertake. But, as much as I recognised her genuine love and concern, her negative, fearful attitude also often annoyed me. I wanted to try new things. I wanted to explore all of who I was and what I could do. I wanted her to encourage me and to boost my confidence and sense of self-worth. Instead, her own anxieties so often seemed to preclude her from being able to do this. In later years, I was grieved for her when I came to realise how much enjoyment she missed out on in her own life because she was seldom able to relax and be at peace.

My father also managed to instil a certain amount of fear in me during my growing up years—but this fear was of quite a different nature. A man of few words and something of a recluse, at times he would lose his temper in spectacular fashion. If I was within earshot when this occurred, it affected me in a profound way. Even if I was not the cause of his angry outburst, I would curl up on my bed with my thumb in my mouth for comfort and cry until the storm was over. On one occasion, I remember how he slammed out of the house and drove off in a fit of rage, as a result of an argument with my mother—or perhaps with all of us.

'B ... *women*!' he spat out, as he headed for the car and revved the engine extra loudly.

A few hours later, he was back, a little shamefaced and perhaps even apologetic, although it seemed beyond him to put such feelings into words. I knew he loved us, despite these occasional tirades over something I viewed as quite trifling. But the fear I experienced at these times was real and did not enhance my sense of self-worth, even if I was not responsible for his outbursts.

This fear and anxiety of mine tended to colour my view not only of myself but also of God. My sister and I attended two different Sunday Schools in our earlier years, before my mother decided we needed to return to the fold and link in with our local Anglican church. Her father had been an Anglican lay preacher and she felt this was where we belonged. On the whole, I did not mind this change, despite the long walk involved on those Sundays when my father was unavailable to drive us. I was confirmed at twelve years of age, as my sister had been, and this seemed to be the signal that our Sunday School days were over. From then on, I understood I was free to attend church, either with or without other family members, whenever I had time. There was no obligation to do so, yet I sensed my mother was pleased and perhaps even relieved when I did.

I did not fully comprehend at that point who Jesus was or what the Gospel was all about. Yet I felt at home in the sacred atmosphere of our church. I believed God was almighty, high and holy, a mystical person far above us whom we were to honour and obey. I remember attending a Good Friday service by myself soon after my confirmation that involved reflecting on the Stations of the Cross. I was the only young person present—and the only one, apart from our minister, who stayed for the entire three hour service. Even back then, something of the sadness of the crucifixion gripped me, as we stood in front of each of the different paintings depicting the Lord's journey to the cross. On the whole, however, God still felt distant and unknowable to me. In my young mind, God was someone who needed placating and who demanded my at least occasional attendance at church. Yet was this some sort of childish superstition I dreamt up myself? Or was this something I took on board from things I perceived in those closest to me?

During these years, my mother attended church when she could.

However, it was her practice to stay home at least every second Sunday morning, in order to prepare a three-course meal for our grandparents who would come for lunch and spend the afternoon with us. If ever I or anyone else commented about her lack of church attendance, she would always be quick to defend herself.

'Listen here! When I was young, we were made to go to church three times every Sunday—early morning, late morning and then again in the evening. So you've got a looooong way to go to catch up to me! I reckon I've paid my dues.'

My father often worked on Sundays, but even when he could have attended church, he usually chose not to. For some reason, church was never a place where he seemed to feel comfortable. One Evensong service we attended as a family remains etched in my mind. There were so few people present that, when the moment came for the offering to be collected, my father was summoned to help. Women, of course, were not asked to do such things then. I can still picture him, as he handed that shiny, brass collection plate around with such awkwardness, then passed it to the minister with all the due ceremony required, before returning to our pew, embarrassed beyond measure. Even though I would have been only ten or eleven, I remember feeling so sorry for him. It was as if he felt too unworthy to be in God's house—and far too unworthy to undertake even the simple task of collecting the offering.

I never knew what his true thoughts about God were in those years, but one day, long after I was married, the picture became a little clearer. We had travelled from interstate to visit my parents during our Christmas holidays when, after a while, my father announced he had to go out.

'Better get going,' he told us. 'Have to be sure to pay God's debts.'

I was puzzled and, after he left, asked my mother what he meant.

'Oh, he's just going down to the church,' she mumbled, looking rather embarrassed.

By then, my parents had moved across town and my mother had begun attending another Anglican church nearby. My father never went with her to an actual service. Instead, he volunteered to mow the grass in the church grounds and take care of the beer bottle recycling bin on the property, put there to raise much needed funds for the church. This seemed to be the way he felt he could 'pay God's debts' and tip the balance in his favour as far as God was concerned. On other occasions, he would also talk about how St Peter might let him inside those pearly gates if he did enough good deeds. Was he only joking? To this day, I am unsure.

I grew up then, knowing some things about God and church that were right and good. Yet I also took on board many fears and fallacies in these areas. If I fronted up at church on a Sunday morning, especially at a Holy Communion service, then I would feel so much more worthy and acceptable to God and so certain everything would go well in the week ahead. If I was able to find the right page in my prayer book and stood or sat or knelt at all the right spots in the service, then I was sure God would be most impressed—not to mention other people seated near me! If I was polite to my parents and teachers, did not swear and always told the truth, then that gave me a much better chance of being in God's good books too. It was all about keeping the rules, about being moral and upright, about looking good—even if I did not feel so good about myself deep inside.

This view of God also impacted my view of the world around me. Somewhere in those years, I decided God did not approve of various people I knew at school or in our street who did not seem to keep the rules in the same way as we did—the man across the road who drank too much, the people whose house was untidy, the dubious family who could not speak English very well and the Catholic folk whose daughters attended Guides with us but could not afford the proper uniforms. Yet our kind, elderly neighbours with whom we often related were Catholic, not to mention my excellent piano teacher. I wondered how it happened that God regarded them as second-rate, but I was glad we were the ones who were right. That had to place us higher up the scale of worthiness, as far as God was concerned. We belonged to the right church. We did the right thing. We lived the right way. Our house and yard always looked right. Therefore, we must be superior to those other people.

I did not realise it then, but God was watching over me, planting those little seeds in my heart that would one day open my eyes to the fallacies I had come to believe and enable me to deal with those fears and anxieties that never seemed far away. When I was around eight, my sister's friend invited us to a children's mission at the small Gospel Chapel we often passed on our way home from school. To my amazement, my mother allowed us to attend every session. I remember how much the enthusiasm of the young man who led those meetings impressed me. He talked about Jesus as if he was his true friend and seemed to believe the Bible with all his heart. Each afternoon, he would challenge us to learn a new Bible verse. If we were able to recite all five verses at the end of the week, he promised he would give us a special prize. Rising to the challenge and, of course, wanting to prove myself, I did just that and received a small, heart-shaped plaque with a Bible verse printed on it in large, silver letters for my efforts. It was Proverbs 3:6 in the Authorised Version:

In all thy ways acknowledge him, and he shall direct thy paths.

I treasured that plaque for many years. Somehow even then, when I still did not understand much about God, I suspect these words reassured me that God would always be there for me, calming my fears and directing my path in life.

I also remember an occasion when our family drove across town to hear the Methodist evangelist, Rev Arthur Preston. My mother's childhood friend had invited us and I suspect my mother felt she could not disappoint someone she had known for so long. Even though I was only young, I loved the earnest, sincere way this minister spoke about God that evening. At the end of his message, when he invited anyone interested to come forward for prayer, I remember how I longed to do just that. I may have even indicated this to my parents, but they seemed eager to hustle me away, scrambling over others in our row as quickly as they could. No doubt it was late and we needed to get home, but I sensed some anger and embarrassment in my parents as well.

And I will never forget the funeral of my old primary school principal which my mother decided we should go to, not long after I began high school. It was held in same small Gospel Chapel where my sister and I had attended the children's mission—our school principal had been a long-time member of the Christian Brethren Assemblies. I looked around the packed church and listened in awe, my skin almost prickling, as most of those present sang with conviction a hymn they seemed to know and love:

> *When all my labours and trials are o'er,*
> *And I am safe on that beautiful shore,*
> *Just to be near the dear Lord I adore,*
> *Will through the ages be glory for me.*
>
> *Oh that will be glory for me,*
> *Glory for me, glory for me*
> *When by His grace I will look on His face,*
> *That will be glory, be glory for me!*[3]

I left that funeral with a wistful heart, longing for this same certainty that one day I would be in heaven, safe and secure forever. How wonderful it would be, I thought, to be able to trust God throughout my life as our school principal had!

Like all of us, whatever our age, I needed to come to know this God who could give me the peace and security I craved and also show me my true worth, which has nothing to do with what we can do but everything to do with what God has done for us. And it was not long after this that God impacted my life in a personal and profound way, dispelling many of the fears and anxieties I harboured, along with many of my false ways of thinking. But this was only the beginning of renewing my mind and heart in God. Since that time, just as Isaiah reminds us to do, I have

---

3   'O That Will Be Glory' (also called 'The Glory Song'), Charles H Gabriel, public domain

learnt I need to continue to focus on God and keep on trusting the One who alone can give us the true peace we all need and desire:

You will keep in perfect peace all who trust you, all whose thoughts are fixed on you! Isaiah 26:3 NLT

At times when I speak somewhere even now, that voice of the enemy who delights to attack us at our weakest points and instil fear into our hearts can be quite loud and incessant, tempting me to respond to the pressures around me in my old childish ways. At times too, when I am in the midst of writing, that same voice will try to plant seeds of anxiety and doubt in me about what I am producing. I have come to see the absolute necessity of keeping my heart and mind centred on God, as I choose to listen over and over again to the One who speaks peace into my life rather than the one who stirs up fear and anxiety.

I have learnt too that I need to close my mind to the idea that God is far too high and holy to be interested in my insignificant writing efforts or any of the challenges I might face in life. I am thankful for those years at Sunday School and church when I learnt to view God with such awe and respect as the Almighty King of Kings, high above us all and far beyond our understanding. But I am also thankful I have now come to know God as an approachable, loving Father, who longs to gather us close and protect us, as Psalm 91 tells us, who forgives us and welcomes us home again, time after time. I know now what I did not know in those growing up years—that I can live in that place of intimacy with our high and holy God, who reigns forever in heaven but who is also with us each day. And I know now I can look to God to tell me who I am, to give my life meaning and worth, to replace those fears with hope and those old fallacies I fell for with solid truth and right thinking.

For reflection

- Write down anything causing you anxiety at the present moment. This is for no one but you to read, so write whatever comes to mind. Sit with what you have written for a while, noticing how your body feels. Take a big breath and try to relax any part of you that feels tense. Remember God is with you and in you. Then read the following aloud slowly:

> *Don't worry about anything; instead, pray about everything. Tell God what you need, and thank him for all he has done. If you do this, you will experience God's peace, which is far more wonderful than the human mind can understand. His peace will guard your hearts and minds as you live in Christ Jesus.* Philippians 4:6-7 NLT

Now spend a few moments in prayer, handing what you have written over to God and receiving God's peace. Then, when you are ready, you might even like to tear up what you have written or get rid of it in some other way.

- In 1 John 4:18, John writes: *There is no fear in love. But perfect love drives out fear, because fear has to do with punishment. The one who fears is not made perfect in love.*

Reflect on this verse for a moment. What does God's love mean to you? Remember, you and I are the reason God sent Jesus into the world (John 3:16). Remember, you and I are so loved that we have been invited into God's very own family (1 John 3:1). How do these truths impact you?

- *For it is by grace you have been saved, through faith—and this not from yourselves, it is the gift of God—not by works, so that no one can boast.* Ephesians 2:8-9

Did you grow up in an environment where you felt you needed to please God and somehow earn salvation? How do you perceive this has affected you?

- There is a choice involved for all of us between trusting God and giving in to fear and anxiety. Sometimes that choice is hard to make. Sometimes we are stronger than at other times. But Jesus does not lie.

And he has said he will give us his peace that passes understanding.

> *Peace I leave with you; my peace I give you. I go not give to you as the world gives. Do not let your hearts be troubled and do not be afraid.* John 14:27

Will you choose to accept this peace Jesus alone can give?

Chapter Four

A Passionate Purpose

"Fear not, for I have redeemed you; I have summoned you by name; you are mine." Isaiah 43:1b

Throughout our childhood years and on into our teens, most of us struggle to discover our identity and to work out where we think we want to head in life. It is a natural part of growing up. And, to a greater or lesser degree, we are all faced with overcoming those fears and fallacies we take on board as children, even in the most perfect of families. Yet, according to our own innate personalities and the impact of others on our lives, we each handle this process in a different way. Some of us cope better than others. But, for most of us, that road to adulthood can become a little rocky at times. So, in order to protect ourselves as we work out who we are, we often develop different layers to our persona under which to hide—our own unique, internal set of Russian dolls, if you like.

As I moved through my growing up years, my own persona came to resemble a type of Russian doll family I have seen only once or twice, where each doll is both similar to but different from the next. There was my bright, happy, 'achiever' persona, for whom things came easily; my good girl persona, who played by the rules and did everything right; my less happy persona, full of anxieties and uncertainties and every-day pressures of homework and piano practice and performing in general; my solemn, quieter persona who liked to hide away and read and dream; and, right in the centre, my smallest, core persona, all curled up, thumb in mouth, wanting to be liked, wishing with all her heart to be popular, wondering what her future would hold, hoping she would be good enough in every way.

By the time I turned fifteen in 1963, I was still unsure what I wanted to do with my life. The time was drawing near when I had to choose subjects at school that would set me on a certain course in my future studies, yet I could not decide which direction to take. At times, I also wrestled with the bigger question of the purpose for my being on this earth at all, although I could not have put it in such terms at that point. By then, I seldom went to church. There was too much else to do, I maintained, which worried my mother a little. I still believed God was to be honoured and held in awe but, for me, other things took priority over wasting a whole Sunday morning at church—things such as doing well in school and music exams, singing in the choir I belonged to and, above all, pleasing myself. Yet, for some reason, when a friend invited me to a weeklong church camp for high school students from across the state in our August holidays, I wanted so much to accept her invitation.

'It's a great camp and the leaders are always good,' she told me. 'Some of our other friends are going too—we'll have lots of fun.'

My heart leapt, then plummeted.

'I'll ask Mum, but I don't think she'll let me come.'

I was convinced of that for two reasons. First of all, this camp was run by the Methodist church and not our own Anglican church, which I thought would worry my mother. Secondly, it would cost what seemed to me a large amount of money and, with only one wage-earner in our family, I suspected that would be an issue.

To my surprise, however, I was allowed to go. This decision was to change the course of my life in a dramatic way and set my feet firmly on the road to becoming the person God had created me to be.

I have now forgotten most of the activities that took place at that camp, but I remember well what happened on the second last evening. We were seated around tables in the large dining room, as we listened to the main speaker, an evangelist in his forties. His words were simple and heartfelt. But what attracted me most was his face, which almost shone as he spoke. God seemed so real to him, so close, so knowable. I wanted with all my heart to experience that same inner certainty about God and that same joy and peace this man seemed to have.

That night, somewhere inside me, a light was turned on.

As soon as he finished speaking, he asked if anyone wanted to make a commitment to follow Christ. Without hesitation, I almost ran to the front of the meeting—the first out of everyone to respond. It was as if all those fragments I had heard about Jesus and God over the years came together in my mind with one satisfying click to form a complete and clear picture, just as when that final piece falls into place in a child's wooden jigsaw puzzle.

Prior to this, I suspect I had decided the things I had heard about Jesus were all good, but perhaps not quite true. If they were, then they did not apply to me on any personal level. Yet now, in an instant, it was as if a veil had been removed from my eyes. I remember thinking, 'Oh, my goodness, Jesus is real! He's alive!' and feeling quite shocked at this revelation. It was as if Jesus had stepped out of one of the beautiful, old stained glass windows at our church and straight into my life. At the same time, I found myself overwhelmed by the thought that I, an insignificant fifteen-year-old, actually mattered to God. How was it possible that such a high and holy God could know *me*, much less love me enough to send Jesus Christ to die for me?

As light dawned in my mind and heart, I knew I had found my purpose for being in this world. It was to live for God—simple as that. Whatever decisions I made about my future career path or anything else in my life, this had to be the bottom line for me.

Later that evening, one of the leaders tried to warn me that things might not be easy after I returned home, but I was still so amazed at what had happened that I did not take in all she told me. I felt so happy and relieved. Jesus was alive in me—I now belonged to him! I did not have the Bible knowledge to understand the exact nature of what had taken place, but when I later read 2 Corinthians 5:17, I realised how well Paul's words described my experience. I was indeed a new creation in Christ. That night, my old life had gone and a whole new life had begun for me.

When I arrived home, I was still floating on air. The following Sunday, I insisted on attending our local Methodist Church, even though my mother was unhappy about it. In my naivety, I thought she would get used to the idea, but that was not to be.

One morning soon after, as I was about to leave for school, I found her in floods of tears.

'What's the matter?' I asked with a sinking feeling, sensing her anger and knowing it had something to do with my Christian commitment.

'I don't want you to go to the Methodist Church and that's that!' she told me, crying even more. 'We've always been Anglicans and that's what you should be too.'

'But ... but it doesn't really matter, does it?'

'Yes, it does matter! You don't have to go running off somewhere else.'

'But we've had the same minister at our church for twenty years! You know how boring it is—and there's nothing there for anyone my age.'

'I know that, but I still don't want you to leave the Anglican Church.'

'Well ... maybe there's another Anglican church nearby where I can go instead. I don't want to stay at our old church. It's just plain dead!'

After many more tears and angry words, I left for school. I was so late, but, for once, my mother did not care because this was such an important issue to her.

In the end, we agreed I should try the Anglican church in the next suburb. At least there seemed to be some life there, despite the fact that, compared to our old church, its services were much more in the High Anglican mould. And, after speaking to the minister and sending me along to talk with him as well, my mother seemed satisfied with this arrangement.

I began attending there on a regular basis. Most Sundays, I found my own way to the 7.00am Eucharist service, after a long walk to the bus stop or train station. One Sunday, I was startled to hear the minister using my own recent conversion story as a sermon illustration, although he did not mention my name.

'A few weeks ago, a young girl came to see me,' he told the congregation. 'She'd had some sort of religious experience at a camp for high school students and wanted to leave the Anglican Church as a result. We talked for a while and I explained to her that she didn't need to race off to some other denomination. Her newly rekindled faith could be channelled along suitable lines within our own church.'

After the service, he apologised in a rather embarrassed yet offhand way.

'I hope you didn't mind my using you as an example. I was going to ask your permission but didn't get around to it. Sorry!'

While I did not mind to any great extent, I was a little taken aback. I also wondered if he had understood how utterly life-changing my experience at the camp had been. Nevertheless, I did as he had suggested and tried to fit in at my new church. I enjoyed singing in the choir, but, while the youngest choir member did befriend me, even she was at least ten years older than I was. I also tried attending the youth group on Friday nights, but soon gave up. I suspect I was much too serious-minded and religious for a group whose main priority seemed to be having fun. Yet several things about this church impacted me in a positive way, including the sense of holiness and awe of God that permeated all the services. I continued to attend there for around four years, but knew in my heart I needed more, if I was to mature as a Christian and grow in my knowledge and understanding of God.

And God provided this much needed nurturing, at first through Crusaders, the lunch-hour Christian group at school, and also through camps this organisation ran in the holidays. Then, in my final year at school, I linked up with the Anglican Church Missionary Society's League of Youth, which met one Saturday night a month. It also ran excellent weekends away that featured good speakers and offered great fun and fellowship. Involvement in a Scripture Union Beach Mission during the Christmas holidays followed, and I also began singing at outreach events run by Campaigners for Christ. Each of these groups taught me much about the Christian life and provided the strong foundation I needed for my faith. I am so grateful for those mature Christians from various denominational backgrounds God put around me who showed me how to be wholehearted in my Christian commitment and inspired me to strive to become more of the person God purposed me to be.

Yet there were disappointments too along the way, as I tried to grow in my new-found faith. The evening I committed my life to Christ, I was given a booklet entitled *Onward with Christ*[4] which contained some daily Bible readings, along with an accompanying encouraging, explanatory paragraph or two. One page I came to re-read often was entitled 'When Christians disappoint you'. Perhaps my expectations of Christians were far too high or perhaps my whole attitude was far too critical and judgemental. But some Christians, it seemed to me, did not live out what they said they believed, which bothered me. At the same time, others appeared to be so rigid and narrow in their beliefs about how Christians should behave—and that bothered me too. I found it all a little hard to fathom at times, yet God continued to enable me to stay true to my commitment and to keep on learning and growing.

At one point during these years, I even found myself drawn to the idea of becoming a nun. At an Anglican summer school I had

---

4   H Bramwell Howard *Onward with Christ* United Church of Canada 1957

been encouraged to attend, I met a young woman who had decided to enter an enclosed, silent order of nuns in England. Her sincere and total commitment to God and her gentle, humble spirit left a deep impression on me. Needless to say, my mother was horrified—and soon my own enthusiasm waned too. Yet, while I put that particular idea aside, by the end of my time at high school, I was still determined to serve God with all my heart in whatever career I undertook. My parents were keen for me to become a high school teacher and, to do so, I knew I would need to complete a Bachelor of Arts degree and a Diploma of Education, as my sister had decided to do. But the idea of pursuing a career in music appealed to me even more.

At that stage, I was still learning the piano. As well, in my second last year at high school, I had taken some singing lessons and had been given a lead role in the school's Gilbert and Sullivan production, an experience I thoroughly enjoyed. Towards the end of my final year, I discussed my future with my English teacher, a committed Christian who was in charge of our Crusader group at school.

'I could go on to university and train as a language teacher, but I'm thinking of trying out for the Conservatorium instead,' I told her.

Her face became grave—she seemed almost horrified at what I had suggested.

'Oh, I think you'd be much wiser to do your Arts degree and teacher training,' she told me in her clear, authoritative manner. 'That way, God could open up all sorts of possibilities for you. By studying music at the Conservatorium, you'd really be narrowing down your options.'

I felt crushed and disappointed, and, from then on, tended to view this caring teacher as a boring spoilsport rather than someone genuinely interested in my welfare. Pursuing a career in music sounded so much more interesting and exciting to me than teaching. What right did she have to squash my music dream out of hand?

Yet, as I thought about it, I had to admit her argument was valid. An Arts degree and teacher training would give me much more of a well-rounded education and a qualification that would stand me in good stead as far as future employment was concerned. On the other hand, carving out a career in music would be a much riskier undertaking. Was there even a chance I could succeed in such a competitive field anyway? My voice was a pleasant, high soprano, but not overly strong. Perhaps too she felt there would be more Christians around me at university and in teaching, whereas the world of music and singing—and opera in particular—might lead me away from the things of God.

In the end, I took this teacher's advice. I chose what I thought then was the safer and more God-honouring option and headed for university. Perhaps this teacher did hear God well and preserved me from exploring a path that would not have brought me any long-term satisfaction or success. Yet, as a result of this decision, I suspect I repressed something at least of the more creative side of my personality, as I endeavoured to succeed in all my uni subjects and devoted much less time to music and singing. Later, teaching was to provide me with many opportunities to be creative and innovative, as I tried to inspire my students and keep them interested in my subjects. But at that point in my studies, my creativity soon became buried beneath the mounds of assignments needing to be handed in with monotonous regularity.

While I may have been ambivalent about my choice of potential career path, I never regretted choosing to become a committed Christian. This decision brought about many changes in my life. It affected not only what subjects I chose to study and how I spent my time but also my whole sense of self-worth and my concept of who I was as a person. Realising I mattered to God gave me much greater security at the very core of my being. Whether I excelled in my studies or not, I knew God would still accept me. Whether I was popular or not with my peers, I knew God would always love me. Even if others did not understand me and rejected me, I knew God never would. In short, I had found that firm foundation on which to build my life and was ready to discover all God had for me to do and be.

Yet that strong desire to please everyone and to be accepted and admired by others did not disappear overnight. After enrolling at university in 1966, I soon became an integral part of the Evangelical Union on campus. I attended our main weekly meetings and also helped lead a lunch-hour Bible study group on the front lawn outside the university's main building, which seemed an all too public spot to me at times. Then, in my second year, I became Publicity Officer for the Evangelical Union. This role involved trying to promote our meetings and events in a variety of ways, one of which was putting up posters in the different faculty buildings, student common rooms and cafeteria areas around campus. I soon discovered what an interesting experience this could be, in an environment where Christians were often regarded as stupid and narrow and thus the butt of many jokes. Yet I knew God was using it to teach me more about myself, as I was thrust into standing up for what I believed.

I also discovered that singing in coffee shop outreach events for Campaigners for Christ and inviting families to activities during Christmas/New Year Beach Missions were not for the fainthearted either. In these challenging situations, I realised my behaviour was still often governed by what others thought of me. I truly wanted to honour and serve God well in all these activities. But I did not always enjoy being viewed by those hostile to Christianity as narrow-minded or naive or even plain stupid for holding onto my faith in God.

As well, my old internal drive to achieve was still very much to the fore during my time at university. I worked hard and tried, in my first year at least, to fit in enough piano practice around my studies and my involvement in Christian activities. In the end, while I failed my associate music diploma, I was determined not to do the same in my academic studies. I had loved studying German at high school, so had decided to major in it, despite the hours of painstaking translation work I knew this would involve. But I soon discovered that Japanese, my other language major, was even more of a challenge, with its different scripts and linguistic structures.

I had decided to study Japanese for two main reasons. Firstly, I loved language learning in general and wanted a second language major. And secondly, I was keen to explore the intricacies of learning an Asian language. I had not been overly impressed when my high school English teacher had talked about the possibilities God might open up for me if I went to university. Yet the thought had already entered my mind that God might call me to missionary service overseas one day. While I sensed even then that Japan was not where I would end up, I decided that the challenge of learning such a complex language as Japanese might prepare me well for learning some other Asian language, should the need ever arise.

In my second year, I added Classical Greek to the mix. I had enjoyed studying Latin all through high school, so was interested to try Greek as well. But I had a second and even more important reason for choosing this subject. I had realised that, if God did call me to full-time service somewhere, I would most likely need to undertake some studies at a Bible or theological college. Choosing to include Classical Greek in my university degree, I reasoned, might therefore help me conquer any New Testament Greek I might need to learn in the future.

In my Classical Greek class, I met a number of committed young men who were endeavouring to combine their theological and university studies. They were seeking to do the opposite of what I envisaged—they hoped their knowledge of New Testament Greek would help them conquer Classical Greek. As I talked with them, I began to wonder whether I could attempt theological studies sooner than I had expected. I had been awarded a Commonwealth scholarship to complete my three year Arts degree. Could I perhaps extend that scholarship for a further two years, in order to complete a combined Arts/Divinity degree? I doubted this would be possible, but went ahead and arranged an interview with the relevant powers-that-be anyway.

As I walked into the interview, I realised with a shock that the man who rose to shake my hand was one of my old high school Maths teachers. I could not believe it.

'Fancy meeting up again like this!' he began. 'What can I do for you, Jo-Anne?'

Feeling so much like that fifteen-year-old student back in his Maths class, I stumbled through my explanation. I wanted him to think well of me, not only because this was something I still craved in any situation but also because I longed for him to view my request in a favourable light.

'Well ... I'm ... I'm wondering if it would be possible for me to change to a double degree and still retain my Commonwealth scholarship. I ... well, I'd like to complete a Bachelor of Divinity as well as a Bachelor of Arts.'

'A *what*?'

'A Bachelor of Divinity.'

'Why would you want to do *that*?'

'Well ... I'm a committed Christian and ... I'm not sure yet, but I think I could end up in some ministry role one day, perhaps even overseas. So I'd like to study any theological subjects I could now while I'm here at uni.'

Later, I wondered if I had misread the look of incredulity and even scorn in his eyes at that point. He listened with what seemed like forced politeness to me, then shook his head.

'No, I'm afraid that can't be done,' he told me, with an almost mocking grin. 'So if you still want this other degree, you'll have to fund it yourself. Now *that* will test your faith!'

I was devastated. I hurried out, fearing I might disgrace myself by bursting into tears in front of him. I knew my parents would be unable to support me through two further years of study without the assistance of a scholarship. So, with great reluctance, I put the whole idea of obtaining a divinity degree aside. Little did I know then that, thirty years later, at an entirely different stage of my life and for quite different reasons, God would see to it that I had the opportunity at last to fulfil my long-held dream of undertaking theological studies.

In my university exams that year, I managed to gain a Distinction in German and Credits in Japanese and Classical Greek. I had become reconciled to the idea of a career in language teaching by then, so continued on with my two language majors, adding Social History as the final subject for my Bachelor of Arts degree. My third year at university was intense, since both German and Japanese demanded many hours of painstaking work. In the last few days of 'swot vac' leading up to my German exam, I almost buckled under the pressure of it all. Had it not been for my sister, who had also majored in German, and the help she gave me in revising my work, I might never have passed. And I was sure I had failed my Japanese III exams.

As it turned out, I managed to pass all my subjects—but only, I am convinced, by God's grace. I can still remember staring at that little word 'Pass' printed alongside Japanese III on the flimsy piece of paper containing my results, my heart overflowing with relief and thanks to God. And I was delighted I had somehow managed to gain a distinction in German. My achiever persona was still very much to the fore and, while I had survived and even benefited from failing my piano exam two years earlier, I had dreaded the thought of tasting failure again. Besides, I would have hated to disappoint my parents and stumble at this final hurdle in completing my Arts degree.

But there was also a further reason for my wanting to pass everything that year. I had become engaged. My life was about to take a whole new direction—a direction which was to allow that passionate purpose God had placed in my heart when I was fifteen to be fulfilled in ways I could never have imagined. I was still hiding under several layers of lack of self-worth, of needing to achieve to feel good about myself, of fear and anxieties, of misunderstandings about myself and God and life in general. But in the midst of it all, I knew I belonged to God. And that made all the difference. I was convinced that, whatever happened in the next stage of my life, my God would be with me, guiding and protecting me as I sought to fulfil my purpose for being on this earth.

For reflection

- Our God is all-powerful and all-knowing, full of wisdom, understanding and strength—the King of Kings and Lord of Lords, so high and holy and so much more awesome than we could ever imagine. Yet you and I matter to him—so much so that he sent his own Son to die for us and to bring us back into relationship with him. As Jesus himself tells us:

    For God so loved the word that he gave his one and only Son, that whoever believes in him shall not perish but have eternal life. John 3:16

    Take a moment to reflect on this amazing act of love that changes everything and shows how much you matter to God.

- *I know that my Redeemer lives, and that in the end he will stand upon the earth. And after my skin has been destroyed, yet in my flesh I will see God ...* Job 19:25-26

    Who will bring any charge against those whom God has chosen? It is God who justifies. Who is he that condemns? Christ Jesus, who died—more than that, who was raised to life—is at the right hand of God and is also interceding for us. Romans 8:33-34

    Jesus Christ is indeed alive—today and forever. How is that truth impacting your life right now?

- Have you ever experienced disappointment with those who claim to follow Christ? How did you handle it? Ask God to give you wisdom and insight as you reflect on any such times in your life.

- As you look back, can you see the hand of God at work in watching over you, bringing the right people alongside you and providing you with the challenges and opportunities you needed to grow as a person and as a Christian? Take a moment to give thanks for God's guidance in your life and for the promise that God's faithfulness will continue on, stretching right into eternity.

Chapter Five
Changing Goalposts

"For my thoughts are not your thoughts, neither are your ways my ways," declares the Lord. "As the heavens are higher than the earth, so are my ways higher than your ways and my thoughts than your thoughts."
Isaiah 55:8-9

There are times in our lives when we shake our heads at where we find ourselves. Sometimes, God opens doors for us that leave us breathless and amazed at the privilege we have been given. Yet, despite our excitement, we may stand trembling on the threshold and wonder if we have what it takes to go through that God-given door. On the other hand, sometimes we find ourselves thwarted at every turn, feeling we may never achieve the things we have dreamt of achieving. Sometimes too, we may even become so overwhelmed with life's challenges that we suspect God has forgotten us altogether.

Later on in my own journey, I experienced all these situations at different stages. But by then, I had realised God knew me through and through and therefore could be trusted to guide me in the right direction at the right time. I did not have to fear. I was in good hands. As a nineteen-year-old student, however, so taken up with the idea of serving God in amazing ways overseas, it came as a great surprise to discover God had something quite different planned for me much closer to home—in fact, right under my nose.

In my Classical Greek class, there happened to be a certain student whose warm, engaging manner, combined with his obvious commitment to the Lord, began to stir my interest. Lionel was in his third year of theological college and also studying four subjects at university. On top of that, he had oversight of a small church as their student minister. Because of all these factors, we did not have time that year to get to know each other on more than surface level. By the beginning of my final year at university, however, I had met his sister, who invited me home one Sunday for lunch. Before long, I found myself helping out each week in the Sunday School at Lionel's church and our relationship developed from there.

I remember the day I felt God made it clear to me that I had found my life partner. Each Sunday, another student minister who worked with Lionel gave me a lift across town to their church. As we arrived one Sunday, I caught a glimpse of Lionel as he stood at the bright pink door of this old, wooden church, smiling and greeting people. The scene seemed to freeze before my eyes and, in that instant, I believed God was showing me in the clearest way possible that I belonged beside Lionel in ministry and in life in general—forever. This was the direction God purposed my life to take.

Yet in the midst of this overwhelming revelation and the joy it brought with it, I also remember feeling a slight twinge of disappointment. I had thought God might call me to serve overseas in some difficult place. I had envisaged completing my degree and teaching diploma, then heading off to theological college and taking up some important role for the Kingdom. I was young and idealistic, so certain I was committed to serving God with all my heart, whatever the challenges. Yet now, via this sudden flash of insight from God, I knew my ministry was to be right here in Australia by Lionel's side. We had not even mentioned the topic of marriage at that point, but, as far as I was concerned, God had spoken—and I believed it would come to pass at the right time.

Not long after, on Good Friday of that year, 1968, Lionel asked me to marry him. We had gone for a drive to a pretty, rural area on the fringe of the city and had stopped the car to relax and chat.

'Oh, wouldn't it be great if we could spend every Friday like this?' I sighed, thinking of the lectures and tutorials that were my usual fare on a Friday, along with working on assignments in the library.

For a while, there was silence in the car.

'Um ... would you ... would you like to spend every Friday of your life like this ... together?' Lionel asked at last, his voice filled with uncertainty.

I did not have to hesitate. Despite his rather oblique question, I knew what he was asking. God had forewarned me, after all. And I knew what my answer needed to be. Besides, it was the answer I wanted to give with all my heart.

'Yes!' I managed to get out, my voice trembling a little.

Again, there was a momentary silence. I waited—and he waited. I could feel the tension in him. Then he cleared his throat and tried again.

'Um ... just to make sure you understand what I'm asking—would you like to marry me and spend the rest of your life with me?'

I felt a little offended he had doubted my ability to understand what he meant the first time around, but I went ahead and repeated my answer, this time in a way he could not misconstrue.

'Yes, of course I would!'

'I ... I just wanted to make sure,' he stuttered, overwhelmed with joy.

Later, he told me he felt like winding the car window down as we drove home across Brisbane and shouting out to everyone we passed, 'She said yes! She said yes! She said yes!'

We were married in January 1969, straight after I completed my degree. Lionel had finished his studies at theological college but still had a few more university subjects to go to obtain his combined Arts/Divinity degree. Thus began a new, steep learning curve for me in so many areas. A week after we were married, I turned twenty-one. And, a few days later, without any teacher training, I took up a part-time role as German teacher at a private girls' school. Meanwhile, Lionel applied himself to his university studies and also continued looking after the small church where he had acted as student minister while at college. The following year, I taught fulltime, after being asked to teach Scripture as well as German, while Lionel took on a fulltime study load at university.

At the end of that year, however, I resigned from my teaching role. I had found it all quite demanding and stressful and we felt it was time for me to have a break. As it turned out, Lionel was offered a position at that same school as a Maths teacher for the following year, while he completed his final university subject.

There were also two further reasons for my leaving. Firstly, I wanted to take up learning the piano again. The rules had changed since I had last attempted to gain my music diploma—I now needed to pass an additional grade before taking this final step. Nevertheless, I decided to try to do this and enrolled at the Conservatorium in some fear and trembling, hoping this would improve my chances. My past failures in my diploma exams still rankled and I was determined to prove I could succeed, as well as justify the cost of all those music lessons my parents had borne over the years.

My second reason for leaving was that we wanted to start our family. Of course, I could have continued to teach while trying to become pregnant, but we felt it was wiser to minimise any physical and emotional stress for me at that point.

Throughout the early years of our marriage, that drive within me to achieve perfection in everything was constant and strong. I had tried my best in my teaching role, but had fought an uphill battle at times, especially with my large Scripture classes. The school where I taught was a prestigious, church-run school, yet many of the girls were unimpressed that Scripture was a compulsory subject in which they were required to sit for an exam. I was determined to teach them something about the Bible, however, and persevered. Yet I found it exhausting, alongside all the preparation required for my German classes. German was a recent addition to this school's curriculum, so there were few resources available and no one to help with lesson planning.

On top of that, as a new teacher, I struggled at times with class discipline. On one occasion, an older, much more experienced teacher emerged from our nearby staff room, disturbed by the noise I was allowing my students to create, and berated me in front of the class. I felt humiliated—it was an effort to hold back the tears until the lesson was over. This event, along with the ongoing challenges of my teaching role, affected my self-esteem and made me feel far from perfect.

I also felt I was less than perfect in my new role as a wife, since, as a result of having to teach every day, I had neither the time nor the energy to keep our flat as immaculate as I felt it should be. I remembered how clean my mother had always kept our home and felt inadequate in comparison. As well, I lacked the time and energy needed to cook those beautiful meals my mother had always produced and that I thought I should too. Lionel was so understanding and helpful, but I continued to cling to my high standards and my desire to be perfect in all areas of life.

Not long after taking up my music studies again, I became pregnant, to our great delight. As a result, my enthusiasm for fronting up at piano lessons and the hours of practice required to meet the expectations of my highly qualified teacher at the Conservatorium soon waned. Once again, I gave up on ever achieving that diploma. In the process, I suspect I disappointed not only myself but also my mother, who had wanted to see me obtain this music qualification so much she had insisted on paying for my lessons at the Conservatorium. Throughout the years that followed, while I played piano or organ at most of the churches where we found ourselves, I often felt somewhat inadequate and wished I could play better. Others seemed to enjoy what I had to offer, but, for me, without that diploma, I was not quite good enough.

After our first beautiful daughter was born in 1971, I was

determined to try to be the perfect mother, doing everything right. I was full of insecurities about this new role, which only added to my general sense of inadequacy in attempting to be the perfect wife and homemaker. I am sure my insecurities affected our baby in those early months, but I stumbled through it all, trying my best. Lionel was constant in his efforts to support me, despite feeling weighed down by a teaching role he did not enjoy at all. And, however inadequate I felt, I was also conscious of God's hand on me during all my anxious moments, strengthening me and never letting me go.

At the end of that year, we faced another big change—leaving the city where I had grown up and where most of our family still lived. After a godly, Christian teacher at school challenged Lionel not to forget his main calling, he decided to return to local church ministry and accepted a position with a small congregation in Sydney. To my parents' great consternation, we were off interstate, taking with us our nine-week-old daughter, their beloved first grandchild.

As time went on, I became more confident as a young mum and enjoyed caring for our daughter and then our son, born in 1973 in our second year in Sydney. I taught Scripture in the local primary school and supported Lionel's ministry in many other ways. Yet I was still that rather insecure perfectionist at heart, always feeling I could do better. And, at times, I was lonely. I read a lot and tried to grow as a Christian. But I did not quite find a home in that local church and was happy when Lionel was successful in obtaining a lecturing position at a Bible college in South Australia. He had already taught some subjects in similar colleges in Brisbane and Sydney and I knew he would find this new role fulfilling and enjoyable. So, once again, we were on the move.

From the outset, we loved our old, stone house in the beautiful seaside town of Victor Harbor. It was the perfect place to bring up our young children, with the beach close by and other beautiful spots only a short distance away along the coast. We ventured out to Granite Island often and climbed The Bluff at Encounter Bay, enjoying the spectacular views from the top. As well, we loved driving through the hinterland area, exploring those winding, country roads that led past dairy farms and orchards where the trees were often laden with apples, pears, stone fruit or almonds, depending on the season.

I took to our life in South Australia with enthusiasm. Relying on memories of my father's gardening, I planted vegetables in the beds we found already laid out in our large backyard. And, still wanting to be the perfect housewife like my mother, I learned how to bottle and also dry the stone fruit growing in abundance on our own fruit trees, how to make jam and how to freeze our surplus vegetables and fruit. I attended sewing classes and joined the local choral society where, for the first time in my life, I took part in performing Handel's *Messiah* and Mendelssohn's *Elijah*, along with various Easter and Christmas cantatas. Most evenings, Lionel had to return to college, about a ten minute drive from our home, in order to prepare for his lectures the next day, but, before he left, he would always read the children a story and help put them to bed. We did not have television in our earlier years in South Australia or even a phone. But I loved those quiet evenings at home, sitting in front of the open fire as I read or knitted or wrote letters to my mother and other family members.

I missed our extended family but was too busy most of the time to feel lonely. And we soon made friends among the college community and at our local church. I taught Sunday school, sang in the church choir and played the organ at times. Yet, while I was a committed Christian, I did not seem to have the energy or even any great desire to spend quality time with God and thus deepen our relationship. I knew I had lost something of the intimacy I had had with God in earlier years, but there were too many things demanding my attention to spend time giving the matter any serious thought.

Around two years after we moved to Victor Harbor, our church held a mission which featured a well-known Christian speaker. During a special meeting held in a friend's home, this man talked about the loving, father heart of God that yearns for us all to realise we are precious children of the Most High King and to walk in that knowledge on a daily basis. I longed for this close, intimate relationship again that he talked about and for the true freedom I sensed was part and parcel of being a child of the King. But I was busy—and I had young children to care for, one of whom was suffering from croup at the time.

The following Sunday, as I stood in the crèche during the morning service, holding our son who was still unwell and listening as best I could, the time came for the Bible reading. It was the parable of the unmerciful servant from Matthew 18. While Jesus told this story to teach the importance of forgiving others in the same way God has forgiven us, this was not the message that impacted me that morning. Instead, all I heard were the words of verse 26, where the servant asks his master, to whom he owes a large amount of money, to be lenient with him:

'Be patient with me,' he begged, 'and I will pay back everything.'

As I heard those words read out, I knew God was saying to me in a firm but loving voice:

This is exactly how you have been treating me, Jo-Anne!

It was as if a knife pierced my heart. Straight away, I saw I was no better than that ungrateful, unmerciful servant. In my mind, I had been saying to God, 'You can wait! I'll come back to you when I'm not so busy and when I'm good and ready!' I felt so ashamed of my attitude. How dare I speak to the King of Kings and the Lord of Lords in that manner? True, heartfelt repentance followed, as I stood rocking our son to sleep in that crèche at the back of our church.

From that point on, I began sensing the presence of God in a new and fresh way in my life. I felt so privileged to be a child of the King and wanted to serve God in a more meaningful manner with all my heart. Around a fortnight later, a friend and I began a women's Bible study group in our home. But before we did, we knew we needed to ask our minister's permission, since this was a new type of ministry for our church.

'Yes, you can run it,' he told us in the end, with obvious reluctance, 'as long as it doesn't degenerate into a gossip session!'

Although I did not quite understand why at that point, I resented his rather patronising attitude and became more determined than ever to ensure this group functioned well from the outset. Each week when it was my turn to lead the study, I spent many hours in preparation, even after the birth of our third child in 1977. I learnt much from the whole experience of co-leading this group, as I tried my best to come to grips with the deep truths of Scripture and share these in a way that was relevant and meaningful to the women present. Even then, I believe, God was shaping me for another ministry role years later in a far different context.

I had so much more to learn about myself, however, and so much more work to do in overcoming those old insecurities inside me. I knew I was a precious child of the King, yet I still needed to live it out more and more in daily life. Twice during our years in Victor Harbor, Lionel had to travel to Fuller Theological Seminary in Los Angeles as part of his Doctor of Ministry studies. Before his second trip, he urged me to come with him for a three week period. At first, I felt I could not leave our children with others, especially our youngest, who was only two years old. However, after talking with a minister friend and his wife who seemed delighted with the idea of looking after a little girl, along with their own three older sons, I decided to go.

At Fuller, I felt privileged to be able to audit a subject called 'Ministry through Small Groups' which Lionel was taking for credit. In the practical component of this course, I found myself assigned to a small group made up of two men and one other woman, all much older and far more experienced in ministry than I was. One day as we chatted, one of the men tried to pay me a sincere compliment.

'Jo-Anne, you're a lovely person,' he told me in his gentle, polite way.

'Oh, I'm not really ...'

He tried a second time, with a little more emphasis.

'Jo-Anne, you're such a lovely person.'

'But ...' I argued again.

The next time, he decided he needed to be even more definite, although his voice was still kind.

'Jo-Anne, look at me! Now hear this and accept it—you truly are a lovely person!'

'Thank you,' I managed to respond at last, embarrassed beyond measure.

I understood what he was trying to do and was grateful he had persevered with me. I knew I still had such trouble accepting any compliment, particularly from a male. But I could not see—or allow myself to see—what this man, a minister and counsellor, appreciated about me. Something in me seemed to whisper, 'But if he only knew what you're like, he wouldn't say such nice things!' Despite my recent spiritual growth, a deep sense of shame and inferiority still lurked under those protective layers that hid the real person inside me. I needed to see myself much more from God's perspective and to allow the person I had been created to be to stand tall and accept such compliments with humility and grace.

At that stage, while I knew I was loved and accepted as God's child, my identity was still very much intertwined with being a wife and mother. Most of the time, I was quite content to allow these roles to define me. But, step by step as God led, I began to realise I also needed to be comfortable in who I was in my own right, to grow much more in my self-understanding and to be honest about what I was thinking and feeling deep inside.

Around three years after we moved to Victor Harbor, a new, younger minister was appointed to lead our church. This man brought with him some fresh ideas and carried out his ministry in a warm, gentle, relational manner. After we had come to know him a little better, he made a comment to me one day that shocked me.

'You must get bored with all of us at times, Jo-Anne.'

'Pardon?'

'You must get bored with us at times.'

'What ... what do you mean?'

'Well, we're all pretty ordinary people. But you've got so much ability in all sorts of areas. You've been to university and studied music and have such a wide variety of interests.'

'No way! How could I be bored with you all? Yes, I've had the chance to study—but that doesn't make me any different from all of you.'

At the time, I felt I was responding with complete honesty, just as I had thought I was with the minister in my group at Fuller Seminary. And at one level, it was true I was not at all bored with the people in our church. I was aware that he and others had not had the opportunity or even the desire to attend university or study music. I had sensed some of them, including him, were puzzled as to how I could be so interested in classical singing and in performing with the local choral society, but I did not judge them for this. To me, it was merely a matter of taste and of different backgrounds. Besides, I saw in this man a much deeper spirituality than I had, along with true Christ-likeness and an engaging humility. I sensed he had many things to teach me, whatever his education or upbringing. In the same way, I had other close friends in that church whose Christian life often challenged me and from whom I knew I had much to learn.

Yet I had to acknowledge to myself later that, on a certain level, what he had said was also true. Sometimes I did feel a little frustrated with those around me who were not interested in the things that interested me. Sometimes I did wish I had friends nearby with a similar academic or musical background. But I chastised myself for having such arrogant thoughts and feelings and pushed them aside. I believed, as I still do, that we all have things to learn from one another, whatever our training or life experience. Yet, in order to live with more honesty and integrity, I began to see the wisdom of acknowledging my true feelings rather than repressing them, while still accepting both myself and others in a loving way.

I suspect this humble, gentle man of God recognised my lack of self-understanding and lack of self-worth more readily than most back then. During a Life Enrichment course he conducted at one stage at our church, we were asked a series of written questions, one of which was: 'Are you in touch with your feelings?'

'Of course I am!' I maintained with vigour in the discussion time that followed. 'I'm very much a heart person rather than a head person.'

Years later, I realised what a pointless question this was. After all, if I was unaware of my real feelings, I would most likely be unaware this was the case! I might well think I knew what I was feeling at any given time—but I might also be deceiving myself. Yet, whatever the limits of this question, God used it to begin to alert me more to my own inner thoughts and responses, even if I was unable to process them any further at that point.

Around this time, my sister moved to Adelaide with her family, in order for her husband to take up a school chaplaincy role there. She had also married a minister and, while we had lived some distance apart in our early years of marriage, we had still remained close via long letters and the occasional visit. At last we were living in the same state again—although only for brief period, as it turned out.

My sister had always shown herself to have a stronger, more independent personality and greater leadership skills than I had. Also, by this stage, she had gained valuable life experience during her years of high school teaching before her children were born. I had always valued her opinion on all sorts of issues and was glad we could now talk more face to face. She seemed to bring a wise, balanced approach to our conversations that I sensed I lacked.

One day when she and her family were visiting us, we found ourselves discussing the topic of roles in marriage.

'Oh, I've stopped disagreeing with Lionel when it comes to making decisions,' I told her at one point, with complete sincerity. 'He always turns out to be right anyway. He just knows a lot more than I do.'

Her jaw dropped.

'Huh?'

She did not say anything more, but her shocked tone and incredulous expression spoke volumes. Later, as I thought about our conversation, I began to see how naive my unquestioning attitude must have seemed to her. It was true Lionel knew many things I did not know. Apart from anything else, he was over seven years older than I was. But, even at that point in my life, I realised what a heavy load I was placing on his shoulders by expecting him to have all the right answers in every situation. We often discussed things and made decisions together, particularly on important matters. But I also believed then that my role as a Christian wife was to be submissive and to allow my husband to lead in all things.

Yet I knew it was not this belief alone that caused me to be somewhat unassertive in our marriage and in life in general. The truth was that I was happy to avoid any real responsibility when it came to decision-making. So often, I did not have the inner strength and courage to stand by my convictions. Instead, I took the easier road of falling into line and agreeing with whatever decision was made. That way, I reasoned, at least I could not be blamed if anything went wrong. Yet, as my sister's shocked response had shown me, I knew I needed to back myself and stand by my own opinions much more often. Yet it would take several years before I would risk taking off those layers of personal uncertainty and gain the confidence required to live and act in a more mature way.

After six happy years in Victor Harbor, we found ourselves on the move again in 1980, when the college where Lionel lectured relocated to Adelaide. But student numbers continued to fall and towards the end of that year, Lionel was retrenched. By then, we had linked in with a local church in Adelaide where I played the piano and sang and also headed up the kindergarten department of the Sunday school, as well as a young mums' Bible study group. Much to the disgust of my new friends there, we decided to move back to Sydney, in order for Lionel to take up a ministry position at another local church. He had loved his college lecturing role and felt it suited his gifts and abilities. Nevertheless, God seemed to be leading him back into a local church setting, so he listened and obeyed.

On the whole, the people at our new church in Sydney were warm and welcoming, But I soon realised I did not fit in as well as both they and I had hoped I would. For one thing, this church prided itself on the many netball teams it was able to field in the combined churches' competition—yet I knew nothing at all about netball.

'You mean you've never played netball—*ever*?' one key leader said with more than a hint of contempt, as she stared at me aghast.

From that point on, I sensed any credibility I might have had with her was lost.

'Never mind,' someone else tried to console me. 'Even if you can't coach or umpire, you can sit on the sideline and hand out the oranges at half-time.'

This was not quite my idea of how best to use my time or my gifts. Soon after, I also discovered I was expected to take on a leadership role in one or both of the women's groups at this church, yet I felt I could serve God much better in other ways. I played piano and organ for our services and also taught three classes of Scripture each week at our local primary school. On top of that, we often had people for meals and were part of a home group. I tried my best in all these areas of ministry. Yet my spirit felt so dry and parched—it was as if I was somehow dying on the inside.

One day, a beautiful lady in our congregation introduced me to friends of hers from another church and the four of us soon decided to form a small accountability group. We committed ourselves to memorising Scripture, praying for one another and holding one another accountable for our general growth as Christians, all of which was so helpful to me. But I still often felt restless and somehow empty. And this feeling was exacerbated in 1983 when our youngest child started school.

By then, I had become part of a local Christian writers' group and had submitted one or two articles to magazines for publication, but that in itself did not fill the hole inside me. I decided to volunteer to teach German to a small number of final year students at our primary school. And I poured my energies into helping our own children with their schoolwork and projects. I am sure I put far too much pressure on them at times, in order to help them succeed and achieve the same excellent results I had always achieved. Yet I knew this was not helpful for our older daughter in particular. Soon after she started school, I had realised she needed to be free to be herself and to do what she felt was her best, irrespective of how I thought she should perform. Now I needed to remember that and to extend that same grace to all three rather than use them to satisfy my own need to achieve or to fill that empty place inside me.

While, on one level, I had quite enough to occupy me, I began to sense it was time to use my brain again. Perhaps I needed to challenge myself in some way, I decided, and to grow again as a person, rather than stagnate. I could not teach in New South Wales high schools because I did not have the required education diploma. Could I try to do something about that? But was it right for me to undertake a course of study that would require hours and hours of work each week? I had always put my husband and children first and was unsure if I had the right to consider doing anything that might prove to be detrimental to their welfare. Perhaps it was better to forget about satisfying my own selfish desires until the children were older.

Yet I soon became even more frustrated and depressed. Lionel was concerned about me and decided to speak with the principal of our theological college, who was also a trained counsellor. After this man had preached at our church one Sunday, we talked with him for a few moments before he left. As we stood together on the grass verge outside our church, he looked down at me from his considerable height and spoke in a kind but firm manner.

'It's time for you to take care of yourself, Jo-Anne. You need to do something for *yourself*.'

I almost burst into tears with relief. In that instant, I felt I had been given permission to step outside the rather restrictive box in which I found myself, breathe some fresh air and move on in my life with a clear conscience. Now was the time to overcome my fear of what others around me might think, to press on towards becoming more of the Jo-Anne I had been created to be and to seek out the next thing God had for me to do.

Once again, the goalposts were about to change in a big way for me.

For reflection

- In Psalm 23:1-3 we read:

    The Lord is my Shepherd, I shall not be in want. He makes me lie down in green pastures, he leads me beside quiet waters, he restores my soul. He guides me in paths of righteousness for his name's sake.

    In your own life, how do you receive guidance from the Lord in making key decisions such as choosing a life partner, leaving a job, changing careers?

- If you have put your faith in Jesus Christ, the Son of God, you have a loving Father in heaven who has welcomed you into the family of God and watches over your welfare. You are a much loved child of the King of Kings! How do you respond to these statements? If you feel you need to, ask God to show his Father heart to you afresh.

- Where are you at right now in your own life? Is it time for you to do something for yourself too? In what way might God want you to be taking better care of your own physical, mental, emotional or spiritual needs?

- Do you think we can lose our own identity at times by investing ourselves too much in the lives of our spouse, children, other family members or close friends? How important do you feel it is to have a strong self-image and a clear sense of our own personal identity?

Chapter Six
Inspired by Love

I pray that you, being rooted and established in love, may have power, together with all the saints, to grasp how wide and long and high and deep is the love of Christ, and to know this love that surpasses knowledge—that you may be filled to the measure of all the fullness of God.
Ephesians 3:17-19

How often we overlook or underestimate the extent of God's love and grace at work in our lives! How easy it is to attribute those moments of breakthrough and revelation we experience to our own cleverness or to someone else's insight or even to pure coincidence and see nothing of God's gracious guidance and provision in it all! Yet, God still perseveres with us, wanting us to experience that full life made available to us through Jesus Christ. With great love, God continues to woo us towards a closer, more intimate relationship, guiding and strengthening us to become more of the person we were created to be.

I believe God's love was evident in those words our college principal spoke to me, encouraging me to do something for myself. I was amazed at how my application to study part-time over two years for my Diploma of Education went ahead without any hitches. And I sensed God was very much with me as I took up my studies at the Sydney Institute of Education, which was then part of the University of Sydney. From the outset, I enjoyed all my subjects and the required reading for our assignments. Having been employed as a teacher years earlier, I felt privileged to be able to reflect on my previous experience in the light of the educational theories and practices I was now studying. While many of the younger students found it so boring and put only minimal effort into gaining their teaching qualification, I revelled in it all.

But there were also parts of my course that tested my resolve to the utmost and caused me to wonder if God's love and grace could in fact sustain me through it all. In my first year, along with my education subjects, I was required to study German Teaching Method. There were twelve students in our class, most in their early twenties. I felt centuries older than them—and it had been many years since I had studied and taught German. In our first lecture, we were asked to introduce ourselves to the group in German.

I almost froze. What had made me think I could do this course at my age? How could God ever save me in this situation? To make it worse, the first class member to share turned out to be a native speaker who seemed to regard us with great disdain. My mind was in a whirl, as I tried to recall the German for certain phrases I needed. I dreaded looking stupid and being judged by them all.

When my turn came, I opened my mouth but then hesitated, paralysed with fear. The silence lengthened. In the end, the lecturer looked directly at me and spoke just three words of German in a kind, encouraging tone.

'Sie brauchen Mut!' ('You need courage!')

He was right. As I stumbled through my introduction, I am sure the courage I so much needed came straight from God. And I found I needed even more of it in the weeks ahead. Yet, as I tried to remind myself, I had one big advantage over the other students—I had taught German before. I remembered how little could be covered in one brief lesson and did not have those unreal expectations that the other students, including that rather arrogant native speaker, had in abundance. Besides, I had children of my own. And I was a determined mature age student, wanting to prove myself to everyone. I was still very much that driven high achiever at heart who aimed to be perfect in everything she did.

In my second year of study, an even more difficult challenge awaited me when I attempted Japanese Teaching Method, along with another group of young students, all of whom had worked in Japan and were reasonably fluent in the language. I had not wanted to take this class—I knew I had forgotten so much of the Japanese I had learnt all those years earlier at university. But I ploughed on, ever the determined achiever, and again, by God's grace, made it through this subject and the practical teaching component that went with it.

Despite the fears and anxieties experienced in these teaching method subjects, I felt myself somehow enlarged on the inside through returning to study and facing the challenges involved. It was hard work, but I had done it. To my great surprise, on graduating at the end of 1984, I was presented with two awards for the highest results in both Principles of Education and Language Teaching Method. I had achieved yet again, although I knew for sure, this time around, that God was the one who had enabled me to succeed. God had a purpose for me and was drawing me on, expanding my vision and showing me more of the person I could become. I felt more alive and alert than I had for some time and ready to move forward into the next challenge God had for me.

At the end of that same year, we found ourselves on the move again, as Lionel had accepted a lecturing position at our theological college on the other side of Sydney. After discovering there was no house available for us on campus, we decided to take the big step of buying our own home. In order for us to cover the mortgage payments, however, I needed to return to full-time teaching. I therefore applied for a job with the NSW Education Department and was soon offered a permanent position as a Japanese teacher at the Correspondence School, but knew I had to turn it down. For once, my lack of confidence was well-founded. My Japanese qualifications looked good on paper, but I was quite aware the reality was different, especially given the fact that many of my potential students would be native speakers. Turning down this job offer meant I was sent to the bottom of the list of those seeking a permanent language teaching position, so I therefore registered as a casual teacher while I waited.

In all this, we marvelled at God's hand on our lives. I had not studied for my education diploma with a view to returning to teaching straight away. All I had wanted was to use my brain again and to find out more of who I was meant to be. Yet God saw to it that, just at the right time, I would have the necessary qualifications to be able to earn a wage and help out with our mortgage. In my first year of casual teaching, there were very few days when I did not work. In fact, some mornings during winter, I would receive phone calls from harassed staff at five or six schools, one after the other, each offering me several days of work. Then at last, halfway through the following year, a suitable permanent position became available for me and I decided to accept it.

Yet my return to teaching brought with it some significant personal challenges. Even when still a casual teacher, I wanted all my classes to be quiet and well behaved. When they were not, I was affronted and allowed it to affect my self-esteem in a drastic way. My expectations were unrealistic, to say the least—I would often be at a school for only a few days, sometimes teaching unfamiliar subjects and with very little support from the permanent staff members around me. No wonder the students did not always behave well in these classes.

Then, after becoming a permanent teacher, I of course applied even higher standards to my own classes. As well as expecting perfect behaviour, I wanted all my students to enjoy the challenge of learning a new language and to work hard. Yet, needless to say, many did not and I was again offended and frustrated. I loved teaching any who were eager to learn. But I did not enjoy the constant battle of keeping my ten large Introductory Language classes in order, as well as trying to inspire my elective students to continue to apply themselves to their studies. Almost every day, I took far too much work home with me, in an effort to maintain the high standard I had set myself, and soon became exhausted.

I also felt I needed to prove myself to other staff members via my hard work and excellent classroom management, since they knew this was my first permanent position with the Education Department. On top of that, as a Christian in the secular environment of a public high school, I did not want the way I taught to reflect on God in any negative way. I felt pressured on every side. I knew that, while some of this pressure was unavoidable and came with the job, most of it was self-inflicted. Yet I could not seem to help myself. I was so prone to taking things too personally, so bent on proving myself, so ready to forget who I was in God and so open to letting others' opinions pull me down.

I believe I would not have survived in teaching as long as I did without the support of friends at the local church we had begun attending. From the outset, we loved the sound preaching and the warm, worshipful atmosphere there. Not long after we arrived, I joined the music team and we soon became part of a vibrant, caring home group. But I also noticed how some of our friends at this church seemed to have more depth to their Christian faith than I did and a much greater sense of the presence of the Holy Spirit at work in their lives.

'What is it you have in your Christian life that I don't?' I asked one couple whose experience of God seemed so much more vital than mine.

'Just wait ... just wait!' they advised, after talking and praying with me. 'God will show you and work in your life at the right time.'

I loved their gentle, wise ministry, but found their advice frustrating. And this frustration mounted after several of our church leaders, including Lionel, attended an interdenominational conference and experienced deep spiritual renewal as a result. I had wanted to attend this conference too but could not because of my teaching job. I felt like an outsider looking in—like a child who gazes with great longing into a shop window full of delicious lollies and chocolates but has no money to buy any. I wanted to taste more of the sweetness of the Spirit for myself, to satisfy that deep yearning inside me. I wanted to discover more of God and, in the process, more about myself as well.

Many times in our home group, I would complain about my teaching job and ask for prayer to survive in the midst of it all. One evening, a young man I loved and respected took the risk of challenging me in his gentle way.

'Are you sure you're in the right job? Isn't there something else you can do?'

I heard him, but could not see any other way to earn the money we needed to pay our mortgage. I felt trapped and exhausted. Then, one Sunday evening after church, I found myself complaining again to one of our ministers about having to face another week of teaching. He looked at me with his rather piercing eyes and sighed.

'How long are you going to do this to yourself, Jo-Anne?'

I burst into tears. I had never thought of my job situation in terms of some sort of self-punishment, yet I saw at once this was the case. In many ways, I was my own worst enemy. I had put myself and my own needs last so often, believing it was right to care for others first, but had taken this to an unhealthy level. As a result, I found it almost impossible to value myself enough to admit I needed to leave teaching and try something else. To make things worse, my pride would not let me. I wanted to succeed in my teaching role. My fragile self-confidence would not let me do otherwise.

Not long after, God intervened in a direct and practical way in my life yet again. Towards the end of 1987, I was offered a job as an assistant editor with a Christian schools' organisation. This role involved preparing and editing classroom material for primary and high schools, as well as producing a small magazine for parents and students. Despite my lack of editorial experience, I accepted the job with alacrity. I found it hard to believe I would be paid to do something I had always loved doing, which was to write. A whole new chapter of my life seemed to be opening up and I looked forward to finding out what God would teach me about myself in the process.

But God had much more ahead for me than my new job. One evening, during a time of fellowship with our church elders and their partners, I shared how much I wanted to experience the same spiritual renewal I had seen others at our church experience that year.

'I would love this to happen right now,' I sighed, 'but I suspect I'll need to wait until I take up my new job next year. I should be able to find more time for God again when I'm less pressured.'

'Lord, we don't want Jo-Anne to have to wait until next year,' one elder then prayed with great earnestness. 'We ask you to bless and renew her *this* year!'

Despite being touched by this man's prayer, I could not envisage any way God would be able to answer it. And, in the busy weeks that followed, I forgot all about what had been prayed on my behalf. But God had not.

After Christmas, our family headed home to Brisbane for a short break. My sister had offered us the use of their house while they were away on holidays. On New Year's Eve, Lionel decided to take our children into the city to join in the celebrations there, but I chose to stay at home. I wanted to be by myself to reflect for a while, as my year came to an end.

As the quietness of the empty house enveloped me, I could feel my mind and body beginning to relax. At a loss to know quite what to do, I wandered over to the piano in the lounge room and began playing some old Scripture choruses I knew from memory. When I had finished, I moved to the centre of the room, as if drawn there by some unseen hand. After a few moments, I opened my mouth and started singing praises to God from the depths of my being in a way I had never experienced before. I continued singing for some time, aware of a deep joy bubbling up inside me, along with great relief that I could sense God's presence around me again at last.

Then, in my mind, I saw an amazing picture. I saw Jesus, holding me as a baby and looking down at me with such joy and delight. As he did, he was whispering over and over again: 'Wow—Jo-Anne! Wow—Jo-Anne!' It was as if I was the most beautiful, perfect baby he had ever seen. I also somehow sensed my first name was enough for him and that he had no real interest in my surname. I was just 'Jo-Anne' to him, so familiar, so perfect—and so loved.

But God had not finished reaching out to me that evening. This first picture was soon followed by a second. This time, I saw a blue baby's blanket edged in satin, with all my awards, school reports and music certificates piled in the centre. Next, I saw two hands lift the opposite corners of the blanket in turn and fold them towards the centre, thereby covering all those reports and certificates. Then these same hands gently slid the resulting bundle to one side of the polished surface on which it was resting. At that point, I realised Jesus was showing me that, while all these achievements of mine were excellent, they did not make any difference to how he viewed me.

As I reflected on both these pictures, I knew without a doubt that Jesus wanted me to see how much he loved me just the way he had created me to be—before I could achieve anything at all in my life.

I stood there for some time, unwilling to move. It was late, but I wanted to rest in that close, loving, accepting presence of God for as long as I could. The profound joy I had experienced as I sang was still there inside me, but now it began to bubble up to the surface in a different way. Soon I found myself laughing out loud—it was as if a heavy load had been lifted from me and I was free again. I laughed for a long time, filled with relief and joy—I could not seem to stop. In the end, I went to bed, but lay there chuckling, as I waited for the family to arrive home. When they did, I called out 'Happy New Year!' to them in a way that must have made them wonder whether I had had a little too much to drink while they were out! Later, I gave Lionel a quick, whispered explanation about what had happened, but it was too difficult for him to take in at such an hour. It sounded incredible even to my own ears, yet I knew every bit of it was true.

At that point, I remembered the elder's prayer on my behalf. Just as he had prayed, I had not had to wait until the new year when my life would be less pressured for God to bring refreshment and renewal. Instead, God had reached out to me in the very final hour of the old year in a way I could never have imagined—and I was so grateful.

Something deep inside me changed that evening, as the successive weeks and months and years were to show. At last I was convinced I was indeed *'fearfully and wonderfully made'*, as Psalm 139:14 says—that God had not slipped up and made some sort of mistake when I was formed in my mother's womb. I had been created in the image of God with great care and was so welcome in this world. I was Jo-Anne, God's unique and precious gift. Others might not accept me, but God did—without my having to achieve anything or prove myself in any way. Others might not love or even like me, but God did. Others might not understand me, but God did. And that was all that truly mattered.

This was a huge step forward in accepting myself and coming to understand the real Jo-Anne inside me who had been hiding for so many years under layers of expectations and self-doubt. If God loved me just the way I had been created, then there must be things within me that were worthwhile and that needed to be expressed in order to bless others in this world. In her book *Invitation to Solitude and Silence*, Ruth Haley Barton writes:

> *When we are settled in God's love at the core of our being, the waters of the soul become much clearer. We glimpse a more authentic self with truer and more essential gifts to bring to the world than those wrestled out of the unconscious striving of the false self.*[5]

At that point in my journey, I was not at all familiar with such terms as the authentic self and the false self. But, in the space of those few brief moments alone on New Year's Eve, I had indeed become settled in God's

---

5   Ruth Haley Barton *Invitation to Solitude and Silence* 2010 InterVarsity Press p 116

love at the very core of my being. I had experienced God's amazing love prior to this—it was one of the key things that had drawn me to God in the first place when I was fifteen. But this time, there seemed to be some fundamental shift inside me as a result—a deep spiritual renewal during which God's Spirit flowed into all those tired, parched places inside me, bringing great healing and refreshment.

After this experience, I was even more eager to learn about the Holy Spirit's work in my life and how I could be empowered to do the things God wanted to do through me. I read books and attended conferences. I talked and prayed with friends on a similar journey. And, guided by our ministers and elders, a few of us explored new ways of moving forward in both intercessory prayer and personal prayer ministry. I learnt much through watching others more experienced and gifted in these areas, as well as through stepping out in faith myself and trusting God to guide.

As I studied Scripture, I also felt drawn to explore the gifts of prophecy and word of knowledge further and to learn how these could enable me to pray for others in a more effective way. These gifts seemed to sit well with my rather reflective, intuitive personality and I soon realised this was no coincidence. Because God knew me through and through, then God was quite able to match my personality and abilities with the spiritual gifts that suited me best. And as I experienced God at work through me in these ways, I grew a great deal in my faith and began to understand better how God could use me to bless others.

Yet I still had some distance to travel in this regard. One Sunday, our music director at church approached three of us who played the piano in our services on a regular basis and handed us each a letter. In these letters, we were told we were released from the music team, without any specific reason being given. I was hurt and angry—I loved being part of this ministry. On top of that, I felt embarrassed. I could see how the remaining pianists on our music team were able to improvise much more freely than I ever would and also play in a more contemporary style. Yet was my playing so bad that I needed to be removed in such an abrupt way? Later, when one of our ministers discovered what had happened, he was angry and wanted to protest on my behalf but, in the end, I decided to let it be. I continued singing as part of the worship team, but soon began to wonder whether I should move on from that ministry as well. What did God want for me in this situation?

I did not have to wait long to find out. One day, the minister who had wanted to protest on my behalf came to me with a challenging request.

'Jo, how would you like to lead worship for our new five o'clock service? Not many people come at the moment, but we hope it will soon grow. I'm sure you could do it.'

At first, his suggestion shocked me. I had never envisaged I would lead worship in any shape or form and felt honoured to be asked, even for this smaller evening service. Part of me leapt at the challenge, but I was also filled with fears and misgivings. What if I made a complete mess of it? What if I did not choose good songs? What if everyone thought I was hopeless? I wanted to say yes but was afraid to.

In the end, I decided to play it safe.

'But ... but I've never led worship before—I don't know if I could,' I blurted out. 'Anyway, why are you asking *me*? I'm sure there are others who would do it much better.'

I could see our minister was disappointed and perhaps even annoyed. After a moment's silence, he looked me straight in the eye, with more than a hint of challenge in his own.

'That's not humility, Jo. That's self-protection,' he told me, with brutal honesty.

At first, I was taken aback. Yet I knew he was a gifted counsellor, as well as an experienced pastor—and I soon had to admit he was right. On the surface, my response had sounded self-effacing and humble—or so I thought. But it was fear rather than humility that had driven me to say what I did. I did not want to open myself up to any sort of criticism or make a fool of myself in front of anyone. While I knew God loved and accepted me, my self-esteem was still a little too fragile to take much of a beating. Even as I stood there, I realised I had to choose between grasping an opportunity to grow or protecting myself from potential failure.

'Okay, I'll give it a try,' I quavered in the end.

I believe this man heard God that day and, in obedience, took the risk of challenging me. I gave it a try and, in the process, soon discovered how much I enjoyed this new ministry. But some weeks later, I was faced with an even greater challenge when I was asked to lead worship in our large morning service. This time, I agreed straight away. And, as I gained more experience, God enabled me to carry out this ministry with a heart to bless others and not to be too concerned about what people were thinking.

Eventually, I came to appreciate what God had taught me through my experience of being removed from our music team. If I had tried to hang onto that role and let my pride get in the way, I would not have been asked to lead worship for our smaller evening service. If I had not been challenged about clinging to my self-protection and urged to say yes, I might never have faced up to myself and my hidden motives. If I had not gained experience at leading worship in that smaller service, I might never have been asked to lead in our large morning service. And if I had not taken up this bigger challenge, I might never have had the confidence to follow God's call a few years later and begin training for ministry. Instead, by saying yes each time and allowing God to peel off more of those protective layers that had covered over my real self for so long, I experienced more growth and fulfilment in my life than I would ever have imagined.

Meanwhile, I had continued on at my editing job—I loved the work and was learning so much. But I soon found myself wanting to become even more involved in the ministry of our own church. God was moving amongst us, challenging us to step out in new and different ways, and it was an exciting place to be. One day, a friend encouraged me to apply for a key administrative position in our Family Resources ministry, the arm of our church with oversight of our child care centre, emergency relief work, Family Support Program and Family Day Care scheme. It had not crossed my mind to do this—I had never worked as a secretary or administrator and felt I did not have the necessary computer and book-keeping skills required for such a role.

'But we'd love you to apply,' my friend told me. 'I'm on the management committee and we believe it's more important to have the right person in this role rather than someone with all the necessary skills. We can employ a book-keeper part-time as well. You're just the sort of person we're looking for!'

I laughed and rejected the whole idea at first. Yet, despite my lack of office skills and experience, I began to sense God leading me to step out of my comfort zone and apply. In no time at all, I had the job.

At the end of 1990, I therefore said goodbye to my editing job and soon found myself seated at the reception desk in our church office. Many challenges lay ahead, as I tried to master the intricacies of my new role and learn how to handle the constant phone calls and steady stream of clients who came seeking practical help. I also inherited a myriad of other jobs—taking devotions for our Family Resources staff, handing out emergency food parcels, praying for people, taking messages for our ministers when our church secretary was unavailable, doing the weekly banking, even mundane tasks such as replenishing toilet paper supplies. I had to be prepared to do anything.

In this role, I always tried to treat those who came for help with the same love and grace with which God had treated me. But this proved to be a challenge at times. After a while, I realised God was dealing with my pride, uprooting long held prejudices and moulding me as only God can. One Sunday evening, as I was helping to tidy up after the service, I saw a man from the local area sitting at the back of our church. This man was well-known to us all because of his drinking problem and also from his frequent visits to the church for emergency relief. That night, unwilling to engage in any conversation with him and assuming he was drunk, I glared at him and continued on my way. But he called out and stopped me in my tracks.

'Hey ... you don't like me, do you?' he challenged, staring straight at me with his vivid blue, bloodshot eyes.

'Yes, I do,' I protested, aware even as the words left my lips how untrue they were.

For a while, he kept staring at me. Then he looked away, laughing to himself. He knew he had hit home with his question—and both he and I knew I had lied with my answer.

I hurried off, leaving someone else to take care of him.

As I reflected on this incident later, I could feel the shame rising up inside me. I had looked down on him, yet I had no idea of his background—how he came to be an alcoholic or whether he had any family who cared for him. I had written him off as the 'no-hoper' I knew my parents would have called him. But I could not get past the fact that this man was loved by God in the same way as I was. He too qualified to be that baby in Jesus' arms, as in the picture I believed God had given me on New Year's Eve. Both of us needed to depend on God's grace to rescue us and to mould us into the people we were created to be. I had no right to judge him. But I had every reason to reach out to him in love.

I have always been moved by the writings of the Dutch Catholic priest Henri Nouwen and by his own personal story. Nouwen, a professor at Harvard Divinity School, left that post at fifty-five years of age to become part of the L'Arche community in Trosly, France. L'Arche is an international network of communities founded by Canadian Jean Vanier, where people with developmental disabilities live together as friends with their helpers. After a year at Trosly, during which Nouwen sought to discern God's leading in his life, he made a long-term move to the L'Arche Daybreak community in Canada. In his book *The Road to Daybreak* that records his inner journey during that year in France, Nouwen writes:

> *[Those with a developmental disability] see through a facade of smiles and friendly words and sense the resentful heart before we ourselves notice it. Often they are capable of unmasking our impatience, irritation, jealousy, and lack of interest and making us honest with ourselves. ... Their heart registers with extreme sensitivity what is real care and what is false, what is true affection and what is just empty words, Thus, they often reveal to us our own hypocrisies and invite us always to greater sincerity and purer love.*[6]

The man who challenged me that evening was disabled in a different way—a way I found difficult to excuse. But I knew God saw into his heart and loved him. And I knew I needed to learn how to do that as well. I was just as disabled by my pride and my judgemental nature and my desire to protect myself. Yet God saw into my heart too and forgave ... and forgave ... and forgave. God was not prepared to leave me as I was but instead was challenging me, in love, to take off those protective layers under which I was hiding, live my life with much more authenticity and reveal more and more of that unique image of God within.

For reflection

- Read the following verses aloud slowly:

    > *I have loved you with an everlasting love; I have drawn you with loving-kindness.* Jeremiah 31:3

    > *How great is the love the Father has lavished on us, that we should be called children of God! And that is what we are!* 1 John 3:1

---

[6] Henri Nouwen *The Road to Daybreak* Darton, Longman and Todd, 1997 p 19

Sit back and try to take in this amazing truth that God ... loves ... you. As you do, can you picture yourself as that little baby in Jesus' arms? How does that feel? Can you hear Jesus saying your name, just as I heard him saying mine? Can you hear the delight in his voice? Take a moment to rest in that love and to experience how real and freeing it is.

- There seems to be a fine line at times between honouring others above ourselves and being too afraid to step out and attempt new or challenging things for God. Have you experienced this fine line in your own life? Which way did you choose to go? Consider also the words of Philippians 2:3-4 and 1 Peter 4:10.

- Reflect on a challenging experience in your life when you may have been embarrassed or offended or even hurt on a deep level. How did God bring good out of this for you?

- What is your personal response to Henri Nouwen's words above from *The Road to Daybreak*?

Chapter Seven

Challenged to Step Out

Trust in the Lord with all your heart and lean not on your own understanding; in all your ways acknowledge him, and he will make your paths straight. Proverbs 3:5-6

God has many and varied ways of leading us on in our lives, growing us in our faith and moulding us into the people we were created to be. This often occurs as we read or hear a passage of Scripture, as was the case when God spoke to me through the story of the unmerciful servant in Matthew 18, when I was a young mum in South Australia. Sometimes, it is the words and actions of others that open our eyes to the truth, as happened to me when our minister friend challenged me about protecting myself and when the man sitting at the back of our church one Sunday evening saw through my hypocrisy. At other times, God may speak straight into our spirit via words or pictures, as I believe happened that New Year's Eve in my sister's home.

But God can also guide in a way that is not instantaneous. Sometimes a vague dissatisfaction may grow within us over a period of time—a desire to be somewhere else or to do something more for God. Often, we cannot quite identify what is happening within us, but as time goes on, we may begin to suspect, sometimes with reluctance and sometimes with a tinge of excitement, that God is stirring us up for a reason and has something different ahead for us.

I enjoyed most aspects of my job at our church but, after around two years, I began to wonder if my gifts could be put to better use in a different role. More and more often, I found myself feeling a little restless as I sat at that front desk in our office, answering phone calls, typing reports and government submissions, directing clients to the right person and doing whatever was needed to support our Family Resources staff in general. At times, a voice inside me whispered, *'You can do more than this, Jo-Anne. Someone else could easily do what you're doing here.'* Occasionally, one of our ministers would tell me he felt I should be working for him and the other ministers rather than for Family Resources.

'You belong on the other side of this office, Jo!' he would say, pointing to the desk where our church secretary sat.

I would shake my head and laugh. I had no desire to swap one administrative role for another. I understood the value of having competent office help for our ministry team, but others were already providing that. Instead, a quite different idea about what God might want me to do was beginning to take shape in my mind.

Because I knew all our ministers well, they would sometimes ask me to pray for them as they passed my desk on their way to deal with a difficult issue or to visit someone in distress. Even if they did not ask, I would often pray that God would guide and empower them in whatever situation they were about to face. But, many times, my heart went out that door with them as I prayed—so much so that, in the end, I had to be honest with myself. I wanted do what they were doing.

At first, this shocked me. How could I entertain the idea of ministry even for a moment? There were so many things that would make such a dream impossible. For a start, I was forty-five years old. And I was a woman. And two of our three children were still living at home. Anyway, how would we ever be able to afford the cost of theological training? Even if we could, would it be a good use of our money at that stage of our lives? And why would I ever think of returning to serious study again? The whole idea seemed crazy, whichever way I looked at it.

Yet it would not go away. In fact, it became even more embedded in my mind. But that old self-doubt, which still seemed to rear its head at any fresh challenge, was also clamouring to be heard. Franciscan priest Richard Rohr, in his book *Immortal Diamond*, writes:

Find God, the primary source, and the spring water will forever keep flowing (Ezekiel 47:1-12; John 7:38) naturally. Once you know that, the problem of inferiority, unworthiness, or low self-esteem is resolved from the beginning and at the core.[7]

God was indeed that primary source in my life. I was convinced God loved me and had created me for a purpose. I knew I had been born again by the Spirit who now lived in me, enabling me to use my gifts to serve God and others. But in my case, that did not do away once and for all with those negative voices within. The enemy had not forgotten how to press those old buttons in my life and how to stir up that familiar uncertainty about myself. Over and over, I questioned what my real motives were in thinking about pursuing theological training. Were they spiritual at all? Did they stem merely from jealousy or a sense of injustice that the men were free to take on a ministry role while women found it so much harder? Had God initiated this idea growing inside me—or was it simply the voice of human aspirations that were far beyond me?

During the Christmas-New Year break that year, before my work at the office began again, I decided I needed to have a personal five day retreat. I wanted to get my thinking straight and try to discern if God was in fact calling me to train for ministry. Friends who lived nearby had gone away for a holiday and were happy for me to use their home for this purpose.

On the third day of my retreat, in the middle of a time of worship, I believe God spoke to me and made my next step quite clear:

---

[7] Richard Rohr *Immortal Diamond* SPCK, 2013 p 14

'You're right in thinking the way you are, Jo-Anne. One day, you will be part of the ministry team at church—so start getting ready now!'

At first, I suspected I had imagined what I had heard. But the words were so precise and held such a note of authority that I felt I could not argue with them. I sat down straight away and began writing a response in my journal:

Lord, I hear you, but I can't imagine our church ever employing a woman—let alone me! I will do what you have said, but I won't tell anyone exactly what that was. I will wait and see what happens.

I came home and told Lionel I felt God wanted me to start studying at theological college, but at that point, I did not tell even him what I believed God had said about my becoming part of the ministry team at our church. We decided the best way forward for me would be to keep working for our Family Resources staff and to audit one subject at a time at college to see how I went. I chose a counselling subject first off and, while I was not required to do the assignments, I kept up with the reading and joined in all the class activities. But it was obvious to me—and no doubt to the lecturer and the other students—how lacking in confidence I was about my ability to return to study yet again. While I enjoyed learning more counselling skills, at times I felt it was all a big mistake, even a sham, and that I had no right to be there, trying to take in knowledge I might never use anywhere at my age.

Yet, despite battling these negative thoughts, I felt sure God wanted me to begin fulltime study the following year. Lionel was not quite as convinced as I was about this, but we decided I should leave my job in our church office anyway. I wanted to spend more time doing all I could to prepare for what God had ahead for me and I also felt led to devote several hours a week to praying for our church. As well, I decided to audit a second counselling subject at college. Now that I had more time, I wanted to glean everything I could from each one of the books on my reading list. I was more interested in learning per se rather than completing the number of pages of reading required for my subject or researching material for any prescribed essay. Besides, I was still unsure whether I would ever be able to complete my whole theology degree, so these course requirements seemed a little irrelevant to me.

I also began to read more about the role of women in ministry and to discuss this with others. Our church did not have any female elders at that point and I soon became involved in asking whether our leaders would consider looking further into this matter. At the same time, I began to reflect more on the role of women in marriage, which, in turn, caused me to become more aware of the dynamics within my own marriage relationship.

Lionel was endeavouring to accompany me on this whole journey of discovering more about myself and of seeking to find who God was calling me to be. At times, I suspect he found my complex nature and my rather impulsive and passionate comments about all the new ideas I was taking in a little overwhelming. Yet we persevered in trying to share our beliefs on these issues, sometimes hitting the mark and sometimes not. In the process, I began to realise how unreasonable it was for me to expect him to understand all my thoughts and desires and to meet my every need. Apart from anything else, our family backgrounds were so different. He had grown up with far fewer privileges when it came to education and pursuing a wide variety of extra-curricular activities. His family had moved around a great deal during his growing up years, which had disrupted not only his education but also any long-term friendships he might have formed. He left high school before matriculating, but returned to study in his twenties, later earning two degrees and a doctorate in ministry. I admired him for all he had managed to achieve and for his determination to fulfil God's call on his life. But I knew it was now my time to walk into more of what God had for me to do as well.

At first, when it became obvious Lionel was still unsure about my beginning college in 1994, I felt resentful and let down. I had wanted to forge full steam ahead with what I was sure God was calling me to do. Yet later, I came to see how God used that year in an amazing way to enable me to crystallise my thoughts in several important areas and to prepare me so much better for what lay ahead. I spent hours praying for our church and beyond. I read a wide variety of books, on top of those linked with my college subject. And I was also able to undertake some important training in prayer ministry.

I loved praying for others at our church and was always amazed and grateful when God gave me some insight into a person's situation, as we talked and prayed together. But I knew I needed to learn more and gain greater confidence in carrying out this ministry. I had heard of Elijah House and the training their team provided, but felt we could not afford the fees for me to attend any of the schools they held at regular intervals. One day, however, a young woman at our church told me she felt God wanted her to pay for me to do this training, which I knew would cost several hundred dollars. I was touched, but also embarrassed. How could I allow her to do that? Yet she was adamant.

In the end, I accepted her generous offer and attended a three week basic prayer ministry school in the first half of that year. I found the teaching so beneficial and biblical and, as it turned out, crucial in equipping me for the many challenging situations I would face in ministry in the years ahead. But it was the small group to which I was assigned as part of the practical component of the course that helped me most. As the five of us in that group discussed what we had gained from our morning lectures, then put these teachings and principles into practice in prayer for one another, God was indeed present amongst us. I received so much personal insight, as well as significant healing, as these four women listened to me, prayed for me and encouraged me in general. In particular, it was their response when I risked sharing with them my dream of attending theological college that I came to treasure above everything else.

'Oh, that's so wonderful, Jo-Anne!' our group facilitator, Joy, exclaimed straight away.

My heart went out to her in gratitude. I had wondered what she would think about this idea, but there was no doubting the sheer delight in her face or in her words.

'You go for it, Joey—you can do it!' a younger woman in the group urged. 'Go on and be that strong woman in ministry! We need people like you. Some of these young guys don't have the faintest idea who they are.'

While these words were like beautiful, healing music to my ears, I still found myself struggling to believe them. But I listened to this young woman in particular, because I knew how much she had achieved in her life through her strong determination to succeed, despite losing her sight as a child, and her firm conviction that God could use her to help others. If she could overcome so many difficulties and continue to pursue her dreams, then I could too, I decided. At that school and in later months when our friendship developed further, she spoke many truths into my life and encouraged me to believe in myself so much more.

Later that same year, I was able to complete the advanced prayer ministry school as well, courtesy of a half scholarship, which further equipped me for what the years ahead would hold. God was watching over me, growing me in confidence and enabling me to realise I did have something to offer as a woman in ministry.

By the end of 1994, Lionel and I agreed I should apply to study fulltime for a Bachelor of Theology and Diploma in Ministry at our college. To do that, I had to obtain the endorsement of our church elders. This involved submitting my reasons for wanting to go to college in writing, then meeting with them face to face. Needless to say, this caused me to feel very vulnerable and unsure. Two others from our church were also undergoing the same process, but they were both young men around the same age as our son. I tried to hold onto the clear call I believed God had given me at my retreat, but it was difficult.

While my friends at the prayer ministry school had responded in such a positive way to my desire to go to theological college, I soon discovered others could be less enthusiastic. On one occasion during this time, we caught up with a couple in ministry who had always been supportive of me in my role as minister's wife at our previous church. I thought they would be so excited about my plans to attend college and could not wait to tell them.

'Guess what?' I began. 'I'm hoping to go to college next year to do a Bachelor of Theology!'

My announcement was met with stunned silence and blank, incredulous stares.

'What on earth would you want to do *that* for?' they said in the end, their voices cold and dismissive.

I stumbled through some sort of explanation, but knew I had not convinced them. The subject was soon changed and the moment passed, yet I was left feeling more than a little dismayed and disappointed. Later, I wondered if they had seen my desire to train for ministry as an attempt to downplay the traditionally important role of minister's wife—or perhaps even as a blatant attempt to compete with the men.

On another occasion, an acquaintance I had met through my involvement in an interdenominational ministry responded with even greater disapproval when she heard of my study plans.

'Oh, what are you trying to prove? I certainly don't need to do that!' she told me in a disgusted tone as she turned her back on me.

Her rudeness stunned me. I tried to dismiss it as some sort of jealousy on her part but, again, it unsettled me.

Then, one Sunday morning, while I was still waiting to hear if my college application had been successful, a visiting speaker came to our church. This man was from a large Pentecostal denomination and was known for giving specific Scripture verses or words of knowledge to those present. After he had finished preaching, he asked anyone who planned to take up some sort of Christian training or Bible college course in the coming year to stand. That morning, I happened to be sitting right down the front where everyone could see me. Was I prepared to stand? Most people did not know what my plans for the new year were at that point. Was I willing to face the inevitable questions and comments that would result?

I risked a quick look around, before struggling to my feet. One or two young people on the far side of the church had also stood, but I decided it was wiser to keep my gaze fixed on the speaker.

'Zechariah 4:6—and 1 Corinthians 16:13,' the preacher said in a loud, authoritative voice as he looked straight at me.

And that was it. The next moment, he had moved on. I tried to remember the references he had given and scrambled to find a pen and paper, but a friend had already torn a page from her notebook and jotted them down for me. To my delight, when I later looked up these verses, I found the following affirming words:

Not by might nor by power, but by my Spirit, says the Lord Almighty. Zechariah 4:6

Be on your guard; stand firm in the faith; be courageous; be strong.
1 Corinthians 16:13

For years after, I treasured that scrap of paper my friend handed me that day. I kept it in the back of my Bible, often reaching for it when I felt overwhelmed in my studies or in ministry. Many times, God reminded me via those verses that, while I needed to have courage and continue pursuing what I had been called to do, I would not have to do it all in my own strength. Instead, God's Spirit would always be working within me to empower me and enable me to keep going.

In the end, our elders endorsed my application and I was accepted for full-time study at our college in 1995—my second time around as a mature age student. This time, however, I had even more reason to be concerned about how well I would go. It was more than ten years since I had studied for my Diploma of Education. Would I still be able to handle the pressure of completing assignments on time, as well as meeting the many other requirements of our college course, including several hours of practical ministry each week? I also knew there would be some required core subjects I would find difficult. I did not feel I had Lionel's capacity for the clear, critical thinking required to do well in subjects such as Biblical Theology and Christian Ethics, for example. Would I be able to manage them? On top of that, the fact that Lionel was the college registrar, as well as one of the lecturers, brought even greater pressure. There was no way I wanted to let him down.

Even more to the point, I did not want to let myself down either.

Before college started, I worked hard to catch up on the written assignments for the two counselling subjects I had already audited, in order to count them for credit towards my degree. I also decided to complete a third subject offered during the holiday period, in the hope of lightening my study load later. Much to my surprise, I received gratifying results in all these subjects. But our minister friend who had earlier challenged me about self-protection had some equally wise words of warning for me in this area.

'Aim to pass, Jo—aim to pass!' he told me, well aware of my perfectionist tendencies and my desire to do well in everything.

I smiled and agreed with him. I knew what he was implying. Yet I felt my eagerness to spend hours researching assignments during my earlier stint as a mature age student had not stemmed merely from my need to achieve. Rather, I had given it my all out of determination to gain maximum benefit from the opportunity to study again. Now, as I began my theological course, I viewed this second return to study as an even more amazing gift. It had been almost thirty years since I had enquired about undertaking a Bachelor of Divinity degree while on my Commonwealth scholarship at Queensland University. I could still taste the disappointment that had resulted from that interview. After such a long waiting period, I was therefore determined to seize the moment and extract everything I could from this God-given opportunity ahead.

Yet it was not long before I discovered my old desire to achieve was still alive and well. As soon as I began to receive distinctions and high distinctions for my assignments, I was determined to maintain that standard for as long as I could. For me, a credit became a disappointing result—almost akin to a failure. Because Lionel was part of our college staff, a few students wondered whether he gave me inside information about our assignments or whether I perhaps held undue sway with our lecturers. Some even wondered whether Lionel helped me with my essays. On one occasion, when a student was bold enough to ask whether this was the case, Lionel responded with humour.

'Oh no!' he told him. 'She wants to do *much* better than that!'

To some degree then, my friend who had maintained I was going to college to prove myself was right. As a mature age, female student, I wanted to show everyone I could do all those assignments—and do them well. On top of that, I wanted to prove to our ministers and elders I could manage the practical ministry roles they had given me. I wanted both the ministry diploma and academic degree on offer at the end of my course with all my heart—and I wanted them with honours. I was thankful our church leaders already trusted me in all sorts of ministry areas. But I also knew I would not be considered for a paid ministry role anywhere without those formal college qualifications. Yet, as far as I could discern, my drive to succeed did not stem merely from a desire to achieve or to challenge the men in their ministry roles. I believed God had called me to train for ministry—and I wanted to do my best to honour that call. I also believed God has a role for women in ministry on an equal footing with men and that I had been given a unique opportunity to demonstrate this. I felt it was important to do so for the sake of other women who longed to train for ministry, as well as for women in general.

I also felt my motives in supporting the nomination of female elders at our church were pure and honest. By my first year at college, our leaders had put in place a process of assessing the congregation's views about this—and it was during this process that my eyes were opened to the vast differences of opinion on the matter. Sincere Christians who all held strong convictions concerning the authority of Scripture still seemed able to reach quite different conclusions about the matter of women in leadership. As our church held further discussions on the topic, I again found my motives challenged, sometimes by those I least expected.

'Be careful this isn't all just a push for power, Jo,' one leader I admired told me, as he gazed at a point somewhere beyond my head and seemed unable to meet my eyes.

My heart sank and my brain whirled. What was behind his comment? Was this his opinion alone or was he passing on a view held by others in our congregation as well? Either way, I felt angry and confused. To me, my integrity was being questioned—and that hurt. I also felt that an important issue which should have been handled with sensitivity and respect was instead being mocked and belittled. Why was it, I fumed to myself, that it was considered a 'push for power' if women with a God-given gift of leadership wished to serve their church as elders, whereas it was a different matter if men wished to do the same?

As I faced these comments about both the issue of female elders and my own decision to head to college, I felt I was being challenged at the very core of who I was. Yet, when I accepted God's call to train for ministry, I had known there would be testing times ahead. On many occasions, I was so thankful for that strong, clear word from God during my retreat about getting ready for my future ministry role. Without that, I suspect I might have shied away from these challenging experiences I encountered and the resultant hours of soul searching.

But God knew it was time for me to grow up, step out and become more of the woman I had been created to be. In the midst of it all, I believed I could trust God to give me the strength to meet these challenges full on. As I was so often reminded through my little piece of paper with the words of Zechariah 4:6 written on it, it was not my own strength or any powers I might possess that would enable me to do what I had set my face to do but rather God's Spirit at work in me. Many times too, I was encouraged as I read the beautiful words of Psalm 139:7-10:

> *Where can I go from your Spirit? Where can I flee from your presence? If I go up to the heavens, you are there; if I make my bed in the depths, you are there. If I rise on the wings of the dawn, if I settle on the far side of the sea, even there your hand will guide me, your right hand will hold me fast.*

I knew the road ahead might not be easy, but I also knew God would be there for me at all times, ready to guide, to comfort and to protect. If I had realised at the beginning the challenges that would lie ahead for me at college and on into my years of local church ministry, I might never have chosen to be obedient to God's call. But, as those challenges emerged along the way, God enabled me to deal with them one at a time and to grow as a person in the process.

For reflection

- Do you agree with Richard Rohr's statement from his book *Immortal Diamond* quoted earlier in this chapter that once we find God, who is the source of living water, '*the problem of inferiority, unworthiness, or low self-esteem is resolved from the beginning and at the core*'? Why/why not?

- How have you handled harsh criticism of your words or actions, perhaps at times in your life when you felt exposed and vulnerable? Is there someone you still need to forgive over this?

- Is there a challenge God is laying before you to take that step of faith into something new and unknown in your life? Could God be inviting you to become more of the person you were created to be? Is there anything stopping you from responding in obedience?

If so, what?

- Proverbs 3:5-6 says:

    Trust in the Lord with all your heart and lean not on your own understanding; in all your ways acknowledge him, and he will make your paths straight.

Take a moment now to acknowledge God's presence with you and to honour him with words or in silence. Then hold out to him that decision concerning your future or that choice you are finding hard to make about some issue in your life. When you are ready, open your hands and your fingers wide and let God take it. In the quietness, listen for that still small voice, speaking peace and reassurance into your heart. Then commit yourself to go on trusting God in it all, even if you cannot imagine what will unfold or cannot see a way forward right now.

Chapter Eight
Learning and growing

Grow in the grace and knowledge of our Lord and Saviour Jesus Christ.
2 Peter 3:18a

Therefore, let us leave the elementary teachings about Christ and go on to maturity ... Hebrews 6:1

It often seems to me that, just when we feel we have arrived and have learnt everything there is to know about ourselves and our relationship with God, our eyes are opened to something else we need to explore or understand. There are fresh discoveries to be made at every twist and turn of our lives, whatever our age—new layers within us that have been kept well hidden over the years and new depths to discover about our God who is so far above and beyond what we with our small minds could ever imagine. At times, we seem to undergo such sudden, internal growth spurts that our lives almost feel out of control. It is as if we are being propelled along through some sort of wind tunnel at great speed, struggling to catch our breath and wondering where we will land at the end of it all—or if we will even make it through in one piece.

This could well be an apt description of my three years of full-time study at theological college from 1995 to 1997 and everything else that went with it. I began my course with a thankful heart, so delighted to be doing something I had wanted to do so many years earlier at university. Back then, I could often have been found sitting with my friends at lunchtime, discussing the big issues of faith and life with all the ignorance and fervency of youth. Now I was forty-seven, with three children who were beginning to find their own way in life. In those intervening years, I had worked in several challenging jobs outside our home. I had explored many issues of my Christian faith and had served in a variety of ministries. Yet there was still so much more for me to discover about God, about the Bible, about ministering to others and, as it turned out, about those different layers pressed down deep inside me as well.

Many interesting challenges awaited me in my college studies. I loved delving into the Scriptures, learning more about the culture and times in which they were written and exploring how the various parts fitted together. I enjoyed tackling New Testament Greek at last and discovering how my knowledge of Classical Greek and even Latin helped so much with this. I felt privileged to be able to think through where I stood on certain moral and ethical issues, both from Scripture and from what scholars had written over the years. I was also glad of the opportunity to study church history, along with subjects such as worship, evangelism, church growth, missions and church leadership. I loved exploring further areas of counselling, learning strategies to strengthen marriages and families and to care for people at different life stages.

In choosing essays to write in all these subjects, I tried to base my decisions not only on how interested I was in a topic but also on which one would most benefit me in ministry. I particularly enjoyed assignments that were of immediate practical use, such as exploring factors affecting the growth of our church, writing a training course for small group leaders or devising studies on surviving mid-life crisis. But all my assignments stretched my mind and deepened my faith. And, perhaps of equal importance, they also enabled me to minister with greater confidence and integrity.

At times, I suspect some other students in my year, along with my supervisors and even the occasional lecturer, thought I was too serious a student, too focussed on understanding all aspects of a subject and on coming to grips with every issue encountered. One of the ministers at our church, who was also one of my supervisors, would often challenge me about this and encourage me to have more fun.

'You need to learn to lighten up, Jo!' he would remind me, with a smile and a twinkle in his eye.

I could see his point. Nevertheless, I enjoyed learning and applying my mind to difficult topics. Sometimes in class, I would question our lecturers about statements I felt were not well thought through. I could not let things pass—I wanted to understand why they believed what they said they believed. One day, to my great embarrassment, I discovered how much this annoyed some of the other students.

'Let it go, Jo!' they told me in the lunch break, as we talked about the particular lecturer we had had that morning. 'You're not going to change his mind, so why argue the point? Just let him get on with it!'

But that was too much of an easy option for me. Besides, I felt our lack of response could well have encouraged this lecturer to continue teaching from what seemed to me far too narrow and rigid a perspective. When we were next in his class, I continued asking questions, albeit in a way I hoped was gentle and respectful. I felt he needed to consider other theological viewpoints and also be less naive in his whole approach to some of the ethical questions under discussion.

'It's just not that black and white!' I commented as politely as I could, given the frustration I was feeling.

Much to his credit, this lecturer managed to remain gracious, although I could see he was a little ruffled. In the end, I did not convince him, just as the other students had predicted, and we agreed to disagree. And at that point, I had to admit to myself that I needed to mature as well in my attitude to those with differing views—including college lecturers. Yet I had seen enough in my life to realise there are times when we have to learn to live with ambiguity rather than work everything out according to some neat system. Even at that stage of my own personal journey, I sensed I was edging a little closer to living out of my 'True Self', as Richard Rohr puts it, and did not feel the need to have everything as cut and dried as this young college lecturer seemed to.

The True Self has knocked on both the hard bottom and high ceiling of reality and has less and less need for mere verbal certitudes or answers that always fit.[8]

All the same, I was the student, with so much still to learn, and not the lecturer. And I needed to remember that.

As a mature age student, I also felt one or two of the younger students in my year were cheapening their whole college experience by cutting corners with assignments and not completing their required hours of practical ministry. While I was endeavouring to wring every last drop of wisdom and expertise out of my time at college, they seemed bent on getting by on as little work as possible. Yet I knew some of them were trying to hold down a job as well as cope with a heavy college and church workload. Others had young families, while my own children were at an age when they could take care of themselves. Even in the midst of my studies then, God was showing me I needed to get rid of my critical, judgemental attitude, learn to understand others better and stop demanding they reach the same exacting standards I so often set for myself.

I was soon to discover further ways I needed to grow in my understanding of both myself and others after I enrolled in a subject called 'The Minister's Personal Growth'. It was presented by the well-known American Christian psychologist Arch Hart and covered a wide variety of spiritual and emotional challenges ministers often face such as depression, anger, guilt, low self-esteem, lack of assertiveness,

---

8   Ibid p 47

role conflicts, sexual temptation, stress and burnout. To my shame, I did not at first appreciate this highly qualified lecturer's input as much as I should have. I decided, in my great wisdom and with my rather idealistic mindset, that none of these issues would cause me any real concern. I was sure, for example, that I would never have a problem with anger. And, while others might suffer sexual temptation, depression and burnout, I could not imagine such things ever happening to me.

Yet, as I listened and reflected more on the books in our reading list, I began to realise how shallow my understanding seemed to be and again, how proud and judgemental my attitude was. I was one of the older students, but I sensed I was nowhere near as mature as I should have been in my thinking and my responses to life in general. It was a confronting experience at times, as I sat with the younger students in our discussion groups and listened to their collective wisdom, to realise how much more personal growth still lay ahead for me.

I suspect our lecturer glimpsed this too in the work I submitted for this subject. For each book on our reading list, we were required to hand in a brief written report. In my usual serious way, I submitted comprehensive, meticulous mini-essays, even going so far as to criticise the lack of editing and repetitive nature of some books, including one our lecturer had written. Not for one moment did I think he himself would read every report we submitted. I was therefore mortified when he returned them to us that very week, all dotted with red comments. What on earth had he thought of my exasperated remarks?

How relieved I was to find only three little words written neatly beside my report on his own book: 'Sad ... but true!' Yet, despite his gracious response, I am sure he could see those not-so-well hidden insecurities that lay behind all my efforts to impress via those book reports and my desire to go far beyond what was expected.

In the main essay set for this subject, we were asked to choose one topic from the course that was an issue in our own lives and to keep writing until we had resolved that particular issue. In other words, we were required to counsel ourselves. I was so sure I could do this that I decided to choose not one issue but three! As a result, I did not plumb the depths of any of them, despite the many words I wrote. In fact, I did not go anywhere near doing that.

One issue I chose to cover was my lack of self-esteem. At one point, I shared how I had received several high distinctions and distinctions for my college assignments and how I knew these good results should serve to increase my self-esteem and enable me to feel confident about my studies. When I received this assignment back, I found Arch Hart had written four words this time in big red letters beside that particular section: 'If you *let* them!'

This brief but insightful comment had a profound impact on me. To my horror, I realised I was still reacting as I had years earlier in the Small Groups course at Fuller Seminary in Los Angeles. Back then, I had been unable to receive the gentle, sincere compliment one of the men had tried to pay me. Now, I could not seem to allow my good college results to affirm me either. Somewhere inside my head, a voice would often whisper: 'You don't deserve these high marks! They're all meaningless anyway. Who do you think you are? You don't know anything!' I knew I had to stop such destructive ways of thinking. And I also needed to be truthful with myself, grow up and accept those good college results with grace and humility. At the same time, I was aware my worth as a person did not rest on my academic achievements—those two beautiful pictures God had given me on New Year's Eve a few years earlier had seen to that. It was high time for me to live out the truths of those pictures more and more in my life and to rest in that amazing love and acceptance only God can offer.

I was thankful in the end that I enrolled in Arch Hart's subject, but I was even more thankful I decided to take a subject entitled 'Women in Marriage and Ministry' in my final year of college. Even the fact that exactly six men and six women enrolled in this class served in a concrete way to reinforce my belief that we were equal in God's sight. Our lectures on the relevant biblical passages about women and how these fitted within the wider framework of Scripture proved to be invaluable, as were the animated discussions that ensued. I also came to appreciate the need to consider the cultural context of Scripture more and to see how this does not undermine the authority of God's Word in any way. All this served to convince me it is not unbiblical to believe women can function on an equal footing with their husbands in marriage, as well as with men in general in ministry. And this conviction gave me greater confidence to stand firm in who I was and to believe I could and should carry out the ministry God had ahead for me.

Without a doubt, my college studies provided me with many opportunities for personal growth, as well as with good preparation for ministry. But the people God placed around me during those years also played a key role. Throughout my college course, I had excellent spiritual mentors, as well as great supervisors for practical ministry and for what was then called integration—that is, integrating the intellectual knowledge I was gaining into my life and ministry and vice versa.

I owe much to my first spiritual mentor, an older woman in our church who prayed for me, kept me grounded and was prepared to challenge me as needed. But the time came when we both felt it would be wiser for me to choose a mentor from outside our church. At that point, I remembered Joy, the facilitator of the small group at my first Elijah House prayer ministry school in 1994, and the way she had affirmed my call to ministry with such delight. I have written in detail in my memoir *Soul Friend* about the rich experiences we shared together in my final two years of college and beyond and how I came to regard her as my wonderful lifesaver.[9] Joy listened as I shared my ups and downs, empathised with me, prayed for me and supported me throughout all the challenges that came my way at college. Together, we

9   Jo-Anne Berthelsen *Soul Friend: The story of a shared spiritual journey* Even Before Publishing 2012

explored the whole area of women in ministry, something about which Joy also felt passionate. Her belief in me and my calling to ministry was foundational for the years that lay ahead, inspiring me to take hold of all God would unfold in my life. And her God-given ability to counsel and pray with me over various emotionally draining issues helped me face the many personal uncertainties that still prevented me from becoming all God purposed me to be.

At the same time, my two supervisors, while having quite different personalities, both contributed much to my personal and spiritual growth. My integration supervisor, with his keen mind and thoughtful approach to ministry, tracked with me with great patience, as I tried to come to grips with one challenging theological issue after another. But his most valuable gift to me lay in the fact that I always felt he treated me as an equal. He was convinced Scripture supported women teachers and leaders in ministry and this firm belief, along with his personal support, encouraged me so much. On one occasion, he called me into his office and handed me a thick, green book that appeared to have seen better days.

'Jo-Anne, we'd like to give you this,' he told me, holding it out with a half smile and a conspiratorial, sideways glance at my practical ministry supervisor who had joined us by that stage. 'I'm sure you'll enjoy what this lady has to say!'

At first, I thought he was teasing me—and when I looked closer at that old book in my hands, I was sure of it. It was called *God's Word to Women: One Hundred Bible Studies on Woman's Place in the Divine Economy* and had been published in 1924.[10] For a few seconds, I contemplated handing the book straight back, if not throwing it at him! The title sounded so old-fashioned and restrictive that I cringed. Such a book, I thought, would be bound to endorse the belief that a woman's place was in the home. So why was he giving it to me? He was well aware of my views on such matters. Was he expecting some fiery,

---

10   Katharine C Bushnell *God's Word to Women: One Hundred Bible Studies on Woman's Place in the Divine Economy* Bushnell 1924

passionate outburst from me?

'Is this a joke?' I asked in the end.

'No, no, I'm serious. I just thought you might be interested to read what this author has to say.'

I was still wary, but thanked him as politely as I could. Later, however, I discovered that the author, Katherine Bushnell, had been an ardent pioneer in supporting women in teaching and leadership roles in the church. She had studied the Scriptures in depth on such topics and had many good things to say as a result. In his own unique way then, my integration supervisor had wanted to encourage me in gaining more confidence as a woman in ministry.

My practical ministry supervisor also provided excellent support for me in the various roles I filled at our church during my college years. In addition, I valued his gentle but persistent challenges to stay close to God in the midst of my studies and not to forget the gifts God had given me in the areas of prayer and prophecy. In my thirst to learn all I could about theology and related matters, he helped me see how my faith could become mere head knowledge, if I did not take care, and how I could end up relying on my own abilities rather than on the Holy Spirit's empowerment. His affirming attitude during our many conversations and his grace-filled approach to ministry in general contributed much to my desire to be the prayerful pastor he believed I could be.

Yet, despite all this support, I still struggled to see myself as someone of worth in ministry, with leadership gifts that could help others grow in a significant way in their faith. To me, the gifted men around me, both at church and at college, seemed to be such capable leaders and to have it all together in ministry, whereas I felt I was floundering in a sea of ignorance and insecurity.

Yet God had this in hand and brought great encouragement to me as a woman in ministry during my last two years at college from two quite different, unexpected sources.

The first of these was a conference for Christian leaders I attended at the invitation of my integration supervisor. As part of the organising committee, he asked me to facilitate a seminar presented by Professor Gilbert Bilezikian, the French-born American pastor, author and Biblical Studies lecturer who co-founded the Willow Creek Church, along with Bill Hybels. I had read his book *Beyond Sex Roles*[11] and loved it. Now I had been given the privilege of introducing him to the many ministers and church leaders packed tightly into that seminar room to hear what he had to say in person on women's equality in marriage and ministry. The fact that my supervisor entrusted me with this task was, in itself, a boost to my confidence. And the simple act of having to get up and speak, albeit briefly, to all those present was an important step forward for me in learning to stand tall as a woman in ministry. I well remember too the moment when, as timekeeper for the session, I had to indicate to Doctor Bilezikian that he needed to finish talking. We had already gone well past the allotted hour.

'I can see our time is up,' he told everyone, with a twinkle in his eye as he gestured towards me. 'She's the one in charge, so I must obey!'

We laughed at his gentle joke, in the light of all he had shared about the equality of the sexes and his own journey in that regard. This touch of camaraderie from such an eminent, Christian gentleman filled me with a great sense of acceptance that remained with me long after the conference was over.

The second important source of encouragement for me as a woman in ministry was a mentor training group I joined in my final year at college, led by an experienced male pastor. This group consisted of eight men and one other woman, most of whom were in some paid ministry role. The entire group accepted me without reservation, even though I was still at college, and affirmed my call to ministry. During one group exercise, one of the younger men present wrote me the following note:

Jo-Anne, I would be delighted to serve on any ministry team you were part of.

---

11 Gilbert Bilezikian *Beyond Sex Roles* Baker 1985

That simple, heartfelt statement meant so much. More and more, I began to realise I had something to offer in mentoring others and in equipping others to mentor, as well as in wider areas of ministry. Each member of this group, including our experienced trainer, fed truths into my life with great patience during the three years we continued to journey together, all of which empowered me to become more of the person God had created me to be.

Halfway through my final year at college, Lionel was retrenched from his position as registrar and lecturer. The college was facing serious financial issues, which necessitated a complete restructuring and the eventual embracing of a different training model. I felt so sorry for him—he had lost a ministry he loved with all his heart and was devastated. For some time, he had also been employed one day a week at our church in a pastoral capacity, but now needed fulltime work and was unsure what this should be.

This turn of events brought much personal anguish for me as well. It was difficult to continue studying at a college from which my husband had just been retrenched. And along with that came the emotional strain of trying to work on college assignments at home while helping a partner through the inevitable grief and loss he was experiencing. But a further challenge emerged for me when it became apparent our church was considering inviting Lionel to become a fulltime member of our pastoral team. If what God had said during my retreat over four years earlier about my joining our ministry team was right, we would then be both colleagues at work and partners at home—and I doubted this would work well for us. While I had grown much more in my own identity, I still had a long way to go and was concerned about how such a scenario would affect our marriage. My approach to ministry was still emerging, but I already knew it was somewhat different from Lionel's. Besides, he had so much more Bible knowledge and so many more years of ministry experience than I did, which left me feeling more than a little intimidated. Would it be wiser, I wondered, for me to find somewhere else to minister where I would have to stand on my own two feet—and where I would also have space to be myself.

In the end, the church elders decided to ask both Lionel and me to join the ministry team for the following year. Lionel accepted, but, after much thought and prayer, I declined. At the time, I felt this was the right decision, despite still believing God had called me to serve on team. Yet my heart was heavy. I loved our church so much.

Not long after, we travelled to the USA to attend a conference and to visit my dear friend from the first Elijah House prayer ministry school I had attended. She had moved to Tennessee, in order to pursue her song writing career. On two occasions during that conference, I sensed God affirming my call to ministry and also challenging me to rethink my decision not to join our ministry team. The first occurred when a speaker invited all ministers present to move to the front of the meeting for a time of commissioning. At first, I found myself reluctant to get out of my seat. After all, I did not know if I would ever be employed in a ministry role. Yet eventually, I felt compelled to step out and join the others—and this decision turned out to be pivotal. As I stood surrounded by a sea of clergy, most of whom were male, I knew God was showing me I belonged alongside them in ministry and that I had something worthwhile to contribute.

The second occurred in a much quieter moment of the conference, after most delegates had left for the evening. As I stood in the darkened auditorium, worshipping with a few others, the presence of God was so strong that I found myself almost unable to move. Then one of the worship leaders spoke to us all.

'I believe some of you had been given a priestly calling from God,' I heard her say. 'Now it's time for you to covenant with God about that.'

Those words pierced my spirit. Again, I could not ignore what God was showing me. My call to ministry was real and I needed to respond, however difficult the road ahead would be.

Later, as we visited my song writer friend who had achieved so much in her own life, despite losing her sight as a child, God used her to affirm my calling as well. Being a fervent supporter of women in ministry, she did not mince words and tried her best to encourage me to become all she sensed I could be.

I returned from that trip then, having heard God's clear challenge to accept my call to ministry and to serve on team at our church, along with Lionel, should this be what the elders still wanted. I felt God had matured me so much in those few brief weeks overseas and was grateful when our church did see fit to offer me a part-time pastoral position for the second time.

By the end of college, I had changed in many significant ways. I had grown on an intellectual level, as I applied myself to my studies and thought through key issues of faith. I had grown on a spiritual level, as I learnt to trust God more and delved further into the Scriptures. But it was on an emotional level that I experienced the greatest change of all. Despite being in my forties, I had still needed to grow up in so many ways. In particular, I had needed to learn to believe in myself so much more and to realise my opinions and my ministry gifts were just as valid as the men's. As I walked out of college on my final day, I felt I had been turned inside out several times over. Yet I knew this time of deep turmoil and change had been crucial for my own personal development, as well as for any future ministry I might undertake. While overseas, I had felt God say to me at one stage:

I know how hard it has been, but I didn't mean to drown you—only to make you more like me.

God was more interested in shaping me as a whole person rather than merely cramming Bible knowledge into my head, I had come to realise. I could not help but agree with some words I read in a commentary on Romans towards the end of my time at college:

God is not so much interested in whether we reach our destination as in how we try to get there. To us the arrival is everything but

> *to God the journey is most important, for it is in the journey that we are perfected, and it is in hardships that he is glorified as we trust him.*[12]

College was indeed a significant journey for me in being perfected and in learning to trust God more. But my arrival at that destination also turned out to be an important event for me. At our graduation celebration, I discovered I had ended up as dux of our year. That achiever part of my personality was still alive and well, I realised, as I sighed with relief that I had come first yet again, despite stiff competition from some of the young male students in particular. But this achievement also served as a strong affirmation to me and enabled me to take up my ministry role with greater confidence. As I accepted my award, I sensed God's hand of grace on me and felt it too in the sincere congratulations I received from the large group of family and friends who had come to celebrate the occasion with me.

I was well aware it was only through God's enabling that I had survived the pressure of such an intense period of study, as well as other significant challenges during those years, including the serious illness of one of our children. When I was invited to speak at our final college chapel service just prior to graduation, the text I chose was Isaiah 40:25-31, with a particular focus on the final three verses:

> *He gives strength to the weary and increases the power of the weak. Even youths grow tired and weary, and young men stumble and fall; but those who hope in the Lord will renew their strength. They will soar on wings like eagles; they will run and not grow weary, they will walk and not be faint.*

I had experienced the truth of these words firsthand throughout my three years at college. I had felt I was running an exhausting marathon at times, but God had prevented me from falling and from giving up. And this knowledge that God could strengthen and sustain me was to stand me in good stead for the ministry years that lay ahead.

---

12   Kent Hughes *Righteousness from Heaven* Crossway 1991 p 291

For reflection

- Take a moment to bring to mind the people who have helped you grow the most in God and as a person. Write their names down and what your relationship with them meant to you. As you do, give thanks for each one and for their impact on your life.

- Have you ever considered finding a spiritual mentor or spiritual companion to help you grow in God? If not, take some time now to pray about this. Ask God to show you someone who might be willing and able to take on this role for you. Alternately, could God perhaps be prompting you to take up the challenge of being a spiritual mentor to others? If so, ask God to show you someone you might be able to help in this way.

- There are different views on the role of men and women in both marriage and ministry, even amongst Christians who hold fast to the authority of Scripture in all matters of faith and conduct. What has shaped your own views in these areas? What conclusions have you come to yourself?

- Would you like to have more knowledge of Scripture and theology or perhaps more ministry training and experience? Or do you perhaps sense you need to undertake some course that will help you understand yourself better? How could you go about achieving this growth you feel you need?

Chapter Nine

Called to Serve

Each one should use whatever gift he [she] has received to serve others, faithfully administering God's grace in its various forms. 1 Peter 4:10

When we know God has called us to do something, we can step out with so much more confidence and joy into whatever the future might hold. We can be sure there will be great fulfilment ahead, as we seek to develop and use our God-given gifts and talents and as we rely on God's strength to do so. Yet even when we are doing what God wants, the road will not always be easy. In fact, we may experience times of great stretching and confusion. The enemy will not be idle when we seek to love and serve the Lord with all our heart. And sometimes, sad to say, we provide the enemy with those perfect footholds in our lives when we lack self-understanding and have not attended to those broken parts within us. Yet how patient and longsuffering God is, always watching over us, rescuing us, reassuring us and refining us! And as we allow God to strip off those protective layers we have held onto for so long, we will find ourselves rejoicing in the freedom of becoming more and more the person we were created to be.

My journey on our ministry team included wonderful times of great joy and fulfilment, but also provided many challenges and opportunities for personal growth. I joined our team in January 1998, still amazed that something I had thought way beyond my reach had come to pass, just as God had said it would. My induction, led by my two college supervisors, had taken place at the end of the previous year because both these men were moving on from our church. They had played a significant role in encouraging me to pursue God's call on my life and I wanted to honour them for that. But now it was time to step out, take my place in ministry and serve God with all my heart. I counted it a huge privilege to be called to work amongst people I loved so much. By then, we had been members at our church for thirteen years and had experienced so much more of God in that time. Some who had played a key role in our spiritual growth had moved on, but many had remained—and I did not want to let any of them down.

I was grateful to our elders for giving me a second chance to join our team and wanted to do whatever it took to repay their trust in me. But I am sure part of my motivation too was to prove I could function as a woman in ministry in my own right, while serving on team alongside my husband. At the beginning of one of my final year subjects at college, the visiting lecturer, after glancing through his class list, had asked us to introduce ourselves.

'Jo-Anne Berthelsen. Oh ... so you're the class "plant", eh?' he commented in a half-joking yet rather sneering manner, when it came to my turn.

I was furious. I sat up straight, glared back at him and responded with some heat.

'Not at all. I'm just a student, the same as anyone else here!'

After the lecture, I tackled him on the matter.

'I'm not here to report on you or anything like that,' I snapped. 'My husband might be on staff at this college, but I'm a bona fide student in my own right.'

His face reddened and he apologised, with a rather sheepish grin. In hindsight, I realised his comment might well have arisen out of his own considerable uncertainty and wariness—I suspect it was his first attempt at lecturing and he wanted to impress the college. But my sharp, defensive response had also displayed a remaining, deep uncertainty about myself. I had wanted to be taken seriously as a mature age, female student. I did not want to be viewed in a different light because I happened to be the wife of someone on staff. And this attitude went with me into my paid ministry role.

With all my heart, I wanted to step out in my own right, yet I still needed encouragement at times to do that and to trust God in the process. My lack of self-worth was an issue I knew I had to continue working on, if this was not to affect my growth as a minister or impact those around me in any negative way. If I did not truly believe I had something to offer in ministry, I might well have great difficulty empowering others to be the people God had called them to be.

Some other ways of thinking I brought with me into ministry also needed God's transforming touch. Looking back, I can see there was a certain level of naivety in me that served to keep me quite ignorant of many things, as I lived in my own idealistic dream world. Yet there was at least one good outcome of this naive attitude. I believe it enabled me to undertake new things in ministry I might otherwise have lacked the courage to try. I did not envisage all the pitfalls that might lie ahead, so how could they deter me? Also, linked to this naivety, was a predisposition to view anything to do with our church through rose-coloured glasses. Yet again, God brought good from this, I believe, because my positive opinion of our church and its leaders resulted in a much deeper sense of unity and trust amongst us. Later, I was to experience some negative repercussions from these personal traits. But at that point, eager to prove myself and so full of enthusiasm and idealism, I threw myself headlong into ministry.

From the outset, I felt respected by our leadership. While I continued on with some of my previous roles, I felt honoured that they trusted me to explore further ministry areas and try to find what suited me best. I continued my involvement in worship leading and also prayer—both corporate intercession and personal prayer ministry. I increased the number of young women I mentored. I took my turn with devotions for our Family Resources staff. I helped lead a recovery course and co-facilitated a grief and loss group. I continued my commitment to promote missions and encourage those we had sent to serve elsewhere. And I devised and conducted short courses to train others in several ministry areas. I also began to preach more often. And there were of course meetings to attend, as well as the occasional wedding, baptism or other special event to prepare for. There was so much to do—and I wanted to be part of it all.

Preaching soon became one of the most fulfilling but challenging aspects of my ministry. Each time I stood at that lectern, I felt I was taking one more giant step towards becoming the woman God had purposed me to be. I loved these God-given opportunities to share from my heart and to watch as the Holy Spirit moved in the hearts of those listening, bringing new insights and fresh hope. Yet I was also aware of the huge responsibility preaching brought with it. Early on, God challenged me never to speak on anything unless it had already been burnt into my own spirit, which made me even more determined to preach with honesty and integrity. I did not want to talk about listening to God, for example, without that being a reality in my own life. I did not want to urge people to be compassionate towards others, if I was not prepared to do the same. I did not want to challenge people to give of their time or talents or money, if I did not do so myself. While some might argue there is a difference between preaching and teaching, I took to heart the words of James 3:1:

> *Not many of you should presume to be teachers, my brothers, because you know that we who teach will be judged more strictly.*

I also took on board the even more solemn warning contained in 1 Peter 4:11:

> *If anyone speaks, he should do it as one speaking the very words of God.*

This verse challenged me, first of all, to give the written Word of God top priority in my preaching. What was my own wisdom compared to the amazing wisdom of God contained in Scripture? Even if my own words fell to the ground, I knew God's words would not—that, as the Spirit worked through them, they would accomplish what God desired, just as Isaiah 55:11 says. But at times, I also began to include brief prophetic words for our church as a whole or for individuals, as God led. I always prayed at length about these, wanting to ensure as best I could that they truly were from God rather than from my own thoughts or imagination. And I always tried to deliver them with humility and grace, yet also with conviction. I wanted with all my heart to speak those '*very words of God*' as I had heard them in my spirit and to encourage others as a result. How blessed I felt when people did respond on these occasions and ask for prayer over the issue God had highlighted in their life! Likewise, I was encouraged whenever God gave me some insight during a time of personal prayer with someone. It was all of God and nothing of me—and I felt humbled to be used in this way.

Perhaps the greatest boost to my confidence in this area of ministry occurred when I prepared and taught a short course on the gift of prophecy. Among those who came was a man I would never have expected to see there. On the day of my induction the previous year, our then senior pastor had asked those present to stand, if they were willing to support me in my ministry. Yet this man had not done so. I could not miss seeing this because he was seated in the second row, right in front of where I was standing. Even then, despite being rather taken aback, I admired his courage.

After the service, he came to me, red in the face and almost in tears.

'I want to explain to you why I didn't stand up,' he told me. 'At the moment, I can't see my way clear to agreeing that a woman should teach or have authority over a man. I don't think that's what Scripture teaches. And I didn't want to be dishonest and just pretend. That doesn't mean that, as I think about it further, I might not change my mind about it one day ...'

I could see how much he hated hurting me. I thanked him for being so honest and we parted as good friends. And almost every time I preached the following year, he would tell me later how much he appreciated my input. I never did discover whether he changed his mind about women teaching men, yet here he was, ready and willing to learn what he could in my short course on prophecy. I valued the good number of women who attended, but his choice to take part served as a particularly strong affirmation to me, as did the presence of several other men. At that point, I still had grave doubts about my ability to contribute on an equal level with the male pastors on our team. I would still often hear that insistent, little voice, whispering its accusing messages over and over inside my head: 'You know the men must be right. They know how to "do" ministry—you don't! Their opinions are much more important than yours.' No wonder I found any affirmation from the men at our church so significant in my journey to becoming the leader God purposed me to be.

Another area of ministry I loved was mentoring. Conscious of the need for wisdom in the use of my time, I was selective about those I mentored, limiting myself to women who showed clear leadership potential and also some giftedness in the areas I knew most about. My aim was to empower these women to rise up and be the leaders God purposed them to be, confident in using their God-given gifts and ready to move forward in ministry. I saw aspects of myself in many of them—the girl wrestling with God's call to serve overseas; the young woman gifted in music ministry, holding down a demanding job in the business world while supporting her husband through theological college; the older woman studying at theological college herself; the young girl with marriage problems, trying to forgive and respond in a good way. I honoured each one of them and found it so affirming to see them step out and do the things God had put on their hearts to do. I could give of myself in each of these mentoring relationships, without thought of being compared to the men on our team. I could be me for God, without restraint. And I found that so rewarding and fulfilling.

I was well aware of the time-consuming nature of such a ministry, yet I believed this was the most effective way I could enable these women to take their place in the Body of Christ and in the world as the leaders God intended them to be. My own spiritual mentor Joy had played such a pivotal role in my college years and on into ministry that I wanted to support and empower others in that same way. I could see I needed to train others to do this ministry as well, however, so that there would be a good pool of mentors available in our church in the future. In my final year on our ministry team, I therefore devised and conducted a mentor training course that sought to raise up twelve people who would understand the value of mentoring and be well equipped to journey with others in this way. Despite being so tired by the time I ran this course, I believe it was one of the most significant ministries I undertook at our church.

My years on our ministry team served to strengthen me so much and to increase my self-confidence, as I saw how God used my gifts and abilities to encourage others. Even in the hard times, I regarded it all as a great privilege and was so thankful for the opportunity to serve God and others in this way. While I often felt inadequate beside my male colleagues, I came to see in the end that there were some things I could do well that they could not. At one stage, when I was explaining to my mentor Joy how unsure I felt about where I fitted in our ministry team, she pulled me up short.

'Jo-Anne, they might need to fit into you!' she told me in her gentle way.

I laughed. It was a novel thought to me. Yet Joy continued to persevere in trying to help me see my worth in ministry and to believe

God had equipped me well for the role I had undertaken. She cheered me on, sharing my moments of joy and fulfilment but also supporting me so well during periods of challenge, disappointment and grief. At times, these came about because of circumstances well beyond my control and with little involvement on my part. Yet, at others, I believe my own personal weaknesses and blind spots contributed in no small measure to the way things unfolded.

One practical example of this lay in the area of my failure to value myself as God did and to see myself in a more positive light. Throughout my time on team, I felt unworthy of the salary the church paid me. Our treasurer was often amazed at my lack of interest in what I earned and how little I understood any pay alterations or leave entitlements she took great care to explain to me. I knew well the words quoted by Paul in 1 Timothy 5:18 that *'the worker deserves his wages'*, but whenever I considered the amount I was being paid for doing something I loved, I would hear that mocking little voice inside my head yet again: 'If only they knew what you're really like! If only they realised how uncertain you feel about things and how little you know, the church wouldn't even think of paying you that much!'

Partly as a result of this attitude, I seldom thought of the hours I put into my ministry role. Both Lionel and I believed that, just as our elders and other key church leaders gave up their spare time to carry out their volunteer ministries, we too should work several extra hours each week unpaid. Yet I often went way beyond that and, since I worked part-time and was at home the rest of the week, this was easy for me to do. Also, I was happy to attend meetings that fell on days when I was not working for the church—or even on our day off.

At one point, I included both Lionel's and my name on the list of people the security company monitoring our church premises could call, should the alarm be triggered out of hours. Mostly, the problem was easy to fix—perhaps a door had been left open or someone had used the wrong alarm code. One evening when Lionel went to investigate, however, he discovered that thieves had smashed in and stolen some kitchen appliances. Yet on several occasions after that, I drove to the church and entered the building alone, after receiving a call in the early hours of the morning. I realised this was unwise and went beyond what anyone would have expected of me, yet I felt compelled to do it. Yes, it was inconvenient and even perhaps dangerous, but these were the very reasons I felt reluctant to ask anyone else to go on that list instead of me.

This unwillingness to expect others to do things was perhaps one of the most serious outcomes of my lack of self-worth. I hated to ask people to do anything that might require time and effort on their part or inconvenience them in some way. After all, if I did, they might not regard me in such a positive light. As a result, I found it hard to delegate tasks that could well have provided others with opportunities for growth and for serving others. But another reason I did not delegate at times was, I am sure, my belief that I could do certain things better than anyone else. At heart, I was still that perfectionist, wanting everything done well so that no one would be disappointed in me or criticise my efforts. In the end, this led to exhaustion and the need to take time off on at least two occasions.

A related issue in ministry for me was my inability to decide where I should focus my energies. I had been involved in so many different areas in the life of our church over the years. How could I let any of them go? Prayer in its various forms was dear to my heart. Missions were my particular passion. I loved leading worship. I placed great importance on mentoring others. The list went on. A further contributing factor to this confusion, I believe, was that I did not know myself well enough and understand where my real strengths lay. And, at times, I was unwilling to listen to the wisdom of others as they observed me in action and to take their comments and advice on board. Yet I knew I needed to do that, in order to find the person God had called me to be and not to go beyond that.

One reason I was reluctant to relinquish some ministries was that there was often no one else to take them on. I could not bear to see things I felt were important fall into a hole or even close down altogether. And I found it hard to watch others suffer as a result of our ceasing to offer a particular ministry. If our recovery course or grief and loss group did not run, for example, the people who needed these would miss out. If we did not continue our various prayer initiatives, who knows how we might go astray as a result of not seeking God's heart? As for pastoral care, if anyone who attended our services on a regular basis was absent for some time, I believed it was important for us to find out what was happening.

'People seem to be falling off the edge of our church,' I would say to my colleagues on team at times, with great anxiety, 'and it's as if no one notices or even cares!'

I felt these responses of mine were legitimate. Yet, underneath it all, there still lurked that childish need to please everyone. I dreaded anyone viewing me or our ministry team in a negative light. I could not bear us to make mistakes or fall short of anyone's expectations or appear uncaring. And I did not want our church's reputation to suffer either. I loved our church so much. I was happy to pour my whole self into serving on team and was deaf and blind at times to certain things God wanted to teach me about myself through others and through the circumstances in which I found myself.

I was forced to reflect more on such things, however, when Lionel sensed it was time for him to leave our ministry team and our church. What was I to do in this scenario? I believed I was meant to stay right where I was. But how could I continue on in my pastoral role and also support my husband, as he tried to discern what God had for him to do next?

This was a huge time of testing for me, as I sought to hold onto the conviction that I had been called to ministry independently of my husband and that my ministry, while different, was of equal value.

By then, I had begun to realise the men did not always have all the answers in ministry, but my sense of inadequacy lingered on. In my naivety, I still tended to place many of the key male leaders in our church on pedestals. I wanted to believe in them with all my heart and was prepared to back them to the hilt. Yet I began to see that, in doing this, I might well be placing heavy, unrealistic expectations on them. And this could only result in disappointment and disillusionment for me, if these expectations were not met. Instead, I needed to believe in myself much more and in what God could do through me. I needed to accept myself as God had accepted me. And I needed to pass this same acceptance onto my colleagues. I needed to take off those rose-coloured glasses and be more realistic about how I viewed others, allowing them the freedom to fail and to make mistakes along the way, while loving and supporting them through it all.

In the end, I remained as part of our ministry team for three more years, while Lionel served in an intentional interim capacity at various other churches, before God made it clear it was time for me to leave too. One night, in the middle of a time of prayer at an elders' meeting, I sensed God speaking to me with great urgency:

'Close the door on this church, Jo-Anne—I have something else for you to do.'

I could not argue, even though I knew my leaving would grieve those close to me and disappoint others who appreciated my ministry. Yet, through these few clear, decisive words, God enabled me to make a choice I could not have made by myself. That night, I felt as if I stepped over the threshold and out of our church, then turned and, with great deliberation, chose to lock those glass doors I knew so well, thus making it impossible for me to re-enter. And as I did, I seemed to stand taller and grow stronger through that one simple action.

At the same time, something within me crumbled and died.

While my last few months on team were some of my most productive, they were also filled with grief, as I prepared myself to relinquish a role I loved and the opportunity of serving a people I loved who had blessed me so much. It was an exhausting yet important part of my journey of learning more about myself and of considering how the real me might look, once the role and responsibilities of ministry were removed. At one stage in those last weeks of ministry, I undertook several sessions with a counsellor, in order to enable me to say a healthy goodbye to everyone, as I was determined to do. Through her insightful observations and her ability to help me express my grief through art, she empowered me to be much more honest with myself. Even at that point, I sensed God was preparing me for another exciting adventure in personal discovery, although I was too exhausted and sad to envisage how that might unfold.

In our final ministry team meeting, each of us took the opportunity to reflect on the things we had learnt in our journey together and to share our dreams for the future.

'I think we all simply grew up,' I commented at one point.

Our senior pastor stared at me and was silent for some time.

'That's so profound,' he said at last—and I could see he meant it.

I am thankful now for all my experiences on our ministry team. Apart from anything else, they provided me with so much more self-knowledge and self-understanding. God was stripping off those layers that had protected who I was at the core of my being for so long—and this process was bound to cause some pain and take many months of reflection to come to grips with. Yet I sensed deep down I was indeed growing up at last and beginning to discover more of who I was meant to be, just as Richard Rohr describes:

> *We do not really find the immortal diamond of the True Self. It gradually appears as we do the work of growing up ...* [13]

I did not want to resist the changes and the reshaping that lay ahead for me. I wanted to discover more and more of those facets of my very own 'immortal diamond' that God had fashioned with such

---

[13]   Richard Rohr op cit p 55

intricacy and care. Whatever cutting and scraping and trimming this process might involve and however painful it might be, I wanted to face it all with courage and do what I needed to do to enable that unique diamond within to sparkle and shine in this world as God intended.

For reflection

- Have you observed instances where lack of self-worth in family members, friends or colleagues has impacted on their relationships with others or on their ability to function at their best in a work situation? How did this unfold and what did you learn for your own life in the process?

- Do you agree that too little self-care and also a reluctance to ask others to do things might be indicators of a lack of self-worth in a person? Why or why not? Have you ever experienced difficulty in these areas?

- Consider where you were at in your life five years ago. What have you learnt about yourself as you have faced life's challenges in those intervening years? Do you respond to such challenges in the same way that you did back then?

- In what specific ways do you feel you need to grow as a person right now? Take some time to reflect on these. Ask God to show you how to move closer to discovering more of that True Self you were created to be.

Chapter Ten

Delving Deeper

Be still and know that I am God; I will be exalted among the nations, I will be exalted in the earth. Psalm 46:10

O Lord, you have searched me and you know me. Psalm 139:1

There are times in our lives when we sail along from one week to the next, busy with all sorts of work, family, leisure and church activities, yet still able to keep things more or less under control. We may even find some quiet moments here and there to be with God, to take in some words of Scripture and to pray for ourselves and others. But we have little time or inclination to step back and reflect on what is happening to us on a deeper, emotional level.

Then we may strike a more demanding period in our lives when the pace becomes frantic and the challenges so draining that we need all our energy merely to stay afloat. We have to fulfil our obligations. We have to set an example to others. We have to keep going. We have to succeed. We have to earn the approval of our peers or of those in authority over us. In the midst of it all, we may come close to disconnecting with God and with what is happening within us on both a spiritual and emotional level. We have no time at all to reflect and, as a result, lose sight of what is most important in our lives. In the end, we may reach a point when things begin to unravel. Then we may find ourselves forced to reassess our lives and to look into the depths of our hearts to see what God is calling us to do and what we ourselves truly want out of life.

If we are mindful of what is happening in our lives on a regular basis and alert to the promptings of God, it is to be hoped we will never arrive at this point. But so many of us seem to plough on, heedless of what we are doing to ourselves. We end up being carried along with the torrent, too absorbed in it all and too focussed on keeping our heads above water, with little strength left to go against the flow in any significant way.

At the beginning of what became my last year of ministry at our church, I believe I qualified well as one of those who plough on, whatever the cost. I loved our church. I felt there was still so much more for me to do there and that it would be unthinkable to lay it all down. Besides, a few months earlier, I had agreed to continue on as part of our team for a further four years. How could I leave now? Yet, if I was unwilling to take care of myself and reluctant—or perhaps even unable—to reassess my life and ministry in a radical way, God was not. Through that clear call I heard to close the door on our church, God ushered me into a period of deep reflection that would see me much more willing and able to swim against that flow and become more of the person I was created to be.

When we belong to God, God takes responsibility for us, just as parents do with their children. In my case, I believe that God, knowing my ambivalence about whether to stay or go, decided to take the initiative and rescue me out of the situation in which I found myself. I did not see this gracious act of God for what it was at the time. Yet I soon came to value the fact that God was not prepared to leave me floundering in deep waters. When I was at my weakest, God stepped in. When I did not know what to do next, God took charge and guided me with great wisdom and understanding and tenderness. I have always loved the words of Isaiah 49:15-16, where God speaks to the Israelites about the restoration of Zion:

Can a mother forget the baby at her breast and have no compassion on the child she has borne? Though she may forget, I will not forget you! See, I have engraved you on the palms of my hands; your walls are ever before me.

This is the same compassion I experienced in my final year of ministry. Despite my slowness to hear and obey and the mistakes I made in that time, God remained faithful. With amazing wisdom and love and grace, God drew me on into the next phase of our journey together.

At my beautiful farewell from our church at the end of 2002, I told everyone I hoped to start writing a book. Yet at that point, it seemed a far-fetched dream—I could not envisage a time beyond that present, sad moment of saying goodbye. And I found it hard to hear all the affirmation showered on me that evening in the form of generous gifts, words of thanks and prayers on my behalf. Many times in the months ahead, I re-read the loving thoughts expressed in the album of cards and personal greetings written by church members and friends and compiled for me with such care. Yet my grief at leaving a place I had loved for so many years prevented me from truly taking them on board and allowing them to affirm me as those who had written them intended.

I also felt guilty and something of a failure that I had walked out of a ministry role I had agreed to fill for another four years. I knew God had called me out of our church, yet I was the one who had made the final decision and had written that resignation letter. All this fed into my lack of self-belief that still lingered on, despite everything I had achieved at college and in ministry and despite all God had taught me about where my true value lay.

Any wonder, then, that the following weeks turned out to be one of the lowest periods in my life. Yet I knew God was there, carrying me and caring for me as only a perfect Father can. Psalm 139, one of my favourite psalms, comforted me so much and reassured me that God knew exactly how I was feeling. I resonated with the words of verses 5-6 in particular:

You hem me in—behind and before; you have laid your hand upon me. Such knowledge is too wonderful for me, too lofty for me to attain.

While I felt I was on the edge of a precipice as far as my future was concerned, gazing down into a black void below, I was also conscious that God was hemming me in on all sides, watching my back, stopping me from falling and guiding me to safety with a gentle but firm hand. I knew the day would come when I would pick myself up again and be able to discern the next thing God had for me to do, but I was too tired even to think about it at that point.

Nevertheless, I soon began to see how God can use these low periods in our lives to enable us to find ourselves afresh or perhaps reveal for the first time that person who has become buried under so many layers of responsibility and busyness and expectation. As those particular layers are discarded, further layers may be exposed that need to be removed as well, with God's help. But adequate time and an uncluttered life are required for such a venture—and I had a whole sabbatical year ahead to take this inward journey with God. I felt so grateful for this time out, well aware not everyone is given such an opportunity.

I realised the most important thing for me to do at that point was to rest. At first, I had no choice in the matter because I felt so exhausted. We enjoyed a brief holiday in New Zealand, although I found I did not seem to have the emotional energy required to appreciate even half of the beauty we saw there. Then my husband needed to return to his ministry role—and, most days, I was left to rest in whatever way worked best for me. Yet part of me wondered how I could do this, when there was so much out there needing to be done for God and for others.

I soon found myself on a steep learning curve in the art of being at peace while doing nothing. This was not new territory for me. Over ten years earlier, I had been unable to resist buying a book entitled *When I Relax I Feel Guilty*[14] because I related only too well to its title. I knew what it was like to be driven by those 'shoulds' and 'musts' the author talked about and to lack that restful, inner peace, even though I might appear peaceful on the outside. In Elizabeth Goudge's novel *A City of Bells*, the elderly Canon Fordyce, while inviting his grandson who has been wounded in the Boer War to stay with him for a while to recuperate, observes with great wisdom:

"It's often necessary in life to do nothing, but so few people do it nicely."[15]

I knew I needed to learn how to rest 'nicely'. I needed to learn just to be—and to feel worthwhile before God as I did.

In all the pressure and busyness of my ministry role, I had almost forgotten the simple but foundational truth I had first come to understand at that camp when I was fifteen—the truth that I mattered to God. Whether I produced anything or not, I mattered because I was created in God's image—and this truth alone gave me so much worth. Of course, there was a time and place for serving God and others as I had been gifted to do, but I knew my sense of worth in this world could not rely on this.

I also remembered the picture God had given me years earlier of Jesus holding me as a baby and gazing down at me with such love, showing me clearly how delighted he was with me, long before I had achieved anything in my life. I recalled too the accompanying image of all my certificates and awards being moved to one side and of sensing how little they mattered to Jesus, compared with who I was at the core of my being. I did not need to feel guilty about not doing anything for God at this point. Instead, I was to rest in Jesus' arms and allow his Spirit to refresh and restore every part of me.

I soon realised too how desperately I needed to learn the art of living more in the present moment. For so long, I had had to think

---

14   Tim Hansel *When I Relax I Feel Guilty* 1981, David C Cook
15   Elizabeth Goudge *A City of Bells* Hodder, 1957 p 24

and plan ahead, as I worked towards completing assignments during my college years and then as I prepared for various church events. Now it was important for me to learn to relax and enjoy what each minute or hour or day brought, rather than allow my mind to race ahead and worry about all the things I had to do. God was in every moment of my day and I needed to be present to whatever God wanted to show me right then and there, even through the most insignificant, everyday things of life.

In order to enjoy the present moment with God, I found I also needed to stop wasting so much emotional energy dwelling on past events I could not change. I still often regretted leaving our ministry team, despite believing God had led me to do so. As I mulled over this decision and the various times when I felt I had failed in my ministry role, I found it so easy to lose myself in a sea of self-blame and negative thoughts. If I had reacted in a different way in this or that situation, maybe God would not have had to tell me to close the door on our church. If I had trained up others and learnt to delegate, my ministry might have been more effective. If I had shown more understanding of team members and lowered my expectations, things might have worked out better for everyone. On and on these thoughts would go, round and round in my head, achieving nothing.

Here was I, now into my fifties, still reacting at times like that much younger Jo-Anne at primary school, hating to fail at anything or to do anything in a less than perfect way.

I knew I needed to deal with these feelings of failure before I could move on to the next thing God had for me to do. In the early months of that year, I tried to identify and confess any ways I might have failed God, then forgive myself and allow God to lift the guilt and shame from me. It was not an easy road and, in my weaker moments, my self-doubt would come flooding back. But I persevered. I wanted to look my real and perceived failures full in the face so they would no longer have any hold over me. And I also came to see that, even if I had failed in certain areas of ministry, it was not the end. Through my failures, I had learnt and grown—and that was the important thing. As David Claydon states:

> *Failures do not determine our identity. Failures are stepping stones, not stumbling blocks. God will enable us to find another way forward.*[16]

To find that way forward, I needed to learn how to be more vulnerable before God, who knew me through and through anyway, as Psalm 139 states. I wanted with all my heart to be real about my struggles and free from any pretence in God's presence. Only then could God remove those layers that still covered who I was at the core of my being—layers such as fear of failure, perfectionism and the desire to have everyone think well of me.

Apart from giving myself permission to rest in God, this was now my key challenge—to discover more about my true self, that most intrinsic part of me. I was no longer a pastor on a church ministry team. I was no longer a teacher or an editor or a secretary or a student. I had no title that described who I was. Yes, I was a wife, a mother, a sister, an aunt, a friend—but these roles all involved a relationship with another person and did not define me as an independent human being. Who was I in my own right? As I stood before God, who was the Jo-Anne I had been put on this earth to be? I felt lost and fragmented, as if I was flailing around like some beached and disoriented sea creature, with no clear goal in mind and no real shape or purpose to my life.

I longed to re-define myself somehow, yet I knew in the depths of my heart I was not to take on another title or role in order to do that. Instead, I needed to remain in that place of rest and just 'be' for a while, without having to be answerable to any boss or organisation. Yet there were times when I found it hard to deal with others' questions about what I was doing, perhaps because they tapped into those I was already so good at asking myself.

---

[16] David Claydon *Who Do I Think I Am?* Morling Press 2013 p 76

'What do you think you'll do next?'

'Why did you bother to do all that study at theological college at your age if you're not going to use what you learnt?'

'You have so many gifts in ministry. Isn't there somewhere else you can use them?'

I hated it even more when friends commented how nice it must feel to be retired. I did not consider myself retired at all—I knew there was so much more inside, waiting to be expressed in some shape or form. I resented any implication that my days of impacting the lives of others were over and that I should perhaps confine myself to supporting my husband in his interim role at another church. Yet Lionel and I both agreed this was not where I needed to expend my energies at that point. I was too exhausted even to think of doing such a thing. Instead, I needed to find my own space where I could focus on the whole process of recovery, as well as on the personal, inner work I wanted to do.

I had embarked on a solitary journey I knew some would not understand. Yet I was not alone. Even in my lowest moments, I was aware God was with me, watching over me, connecting me with those who would provide me with the encouragement I needed. I knew God loved me with an amazing love that is too wonderful to comprehend fully, as Paul reminds us in Ephesians 3:18-19. I believed God could be trusted to reveal to me the truth about myself and to show me the way ahead. I sensed I had the freedom to explore new paths, think new thoughts and no doubt take some wrong turns along the way. Yet I knew God would always be there for me, enabling me to stand firm on that Rock who is Jesus Christ wherever I wandered and leading me all the while in the right direction.

As my sabbatical year unfolded, I chose to undertake an interesting course entitled 'Developing Your Own Spirituality', conducted at the Aquinas Academy in the city. This course enabled me to look at my faith from a somewhat different perspective and explore many of the basic, life-changing truths of Christianity all over again. I also appreciated the discussion group I joined as part of this course and the gracious, observant nun who led us each week. Through this group, I began to see afresh the God-given gifts I had to offer others as a woman in ministry. At the end of our final time together, our leader chose to ask me rather than one of the nuns in the group to pray a blessing over us all. As I heard her gentle request and did as she asked, I felt I had received a wonderful gift. It was as if God said to me:

> 'You can stand tall, Jo-Anne, as a woman in ministry. See how these dear ones from other parts of the Body of Christ have acknowledged your strong faith in me and your obvious call to minister to others. Go forward with your head held high to face the next challenge I have for you!'

This course also inspired me to read some of the writings of the early theologians and desert fathers, along with mystics such as John of the Cross, Teresa of Avila and Julian of Norwich. I was well aware I was scratching only the surface of their work but learnt much from those portions I was able to read. Such writings seemed to speak to and affirm that more contemplative, reflective part of my personality I had ignored for too long. How healing it was to sit and read these often simple yet profound thoughts written so long ago and to realise how they could still impact us here and now! At times, I still felt guilty about the many hours I spent in reading and reflection, not producing anything others could see. Yet I knew God was working in me to bring about more fruit in the next season of my life—a season when, by God's grace, I too could perhaps leave a lasting impact in the lives of others.

In this time, I also chose to read books by a wide variety of authors representing a wide variety of genres. I delved into an eclectic mix of novels and biographies and also enjoyed exploring the works of interesting writers such as Simone Weil, Thomas Merton, Annie Dillard and Flannery O'Connor. Other Christian authors such as Frederick Buechner, Henri Nouwen, Joan Chittister and Vinita Hampton Wright came to my attention too, often during conversations with my mentor Joy or via a quote or footnote in a book. All these fed my spirit, often providing me with fresh, valuable revelations about God and about myself.

While some of my Christian friends did not read such authors and perhaps even dismissed much of their works, I decided to trust God to show me what parts of their rich writings I needed to take on board and what I could set aside or perhaps revisit at a later stage. As I read and reflected, I felt my spirit being enlarged and enlivened. Some of these authors gave me a sense of rightness about myself that came almost as a relief. It was wonderful to feel validated in this way and to read thoughts I myself had wanted to express for so long, but could not find the words to do so. I also admired the individuality of these writers and their ability to express their faith in such beautiful, eloquent and, at times, unusual ways. This, in turn, encouraged me to try to express more of what was inside me. God was in it all, I realised—and I was so grateful.

I also spent time reflecting on my personality type and how I tend to respond to God, to others and to the world around me. I was well aware of the possible danger of becoming too narcissistic and navel-gazing in the process. Yet I felt compelled to continue this soul-searching, in order to allow God to show me aspects of myself I might otherwise have been tempted to hide or perhaps de-value. Sometimes God highlighted these things as I read books and articles about the various personality types or reflected on a passage of Scripture. At other times, enlightenment would come through discussions with family and friends. These were humbling experiences, as I identified certain weaknesses within me and in the way I related to others. I often felt a little like the Canadian theologian Jean Vanier, founder of the L'Arche communities for the disabled, who wrote during his own journey of discovery:

> *That, I think, was what caused me the most pain: to discover who I really am, and to realize that maybe I did not want to know who I really was! I did not want to admit all the garbage inside me.*[17]

But I also unearthed some personal strengths in me that I had not

---

17   Jean Vanier *From Brokenness to Community* Paulist Press 1992 p 19

acknowledged as such in the past. In the process, I became more honest with myself and accepting of the unique person God had created me to be. Little by little, I felt more able to own my God-given gifts and abilities and to stop comparing myself to others, especially the men I knew and had worked with in ministry. Along with this, I began to appreciate my own unique store of personal wisdom, gained from years of experience in different roles, and to realise this too was to be treasured as a gift from God. My responsibility before God, I came to see, was to be all of me in this world, rather than waste time trying to be anyone else. As God led, I was learning to leave behind more of what Thomas Merton, Richard Rohr and others have termed that 'false self' and to uncover my 'true self'—that authentic person I was created to be who could reflect the image of God to those around me in my own unique way.

At some stage in our lives, I believe we all need to make this journey of finding out who we are and of taking off those layers that keep our true self safe and hidden. Some people seem to arrive at this self-knowledge much earlier than others and with less pain and effort. On the other hand, some reach the end of their lives without ever discovering who they truly are. John Ortberg, in his book *Soul Keeping*, tells how he came to ask himself several honest, life-changing questions in this regard:

Why am I never satisfied? Why do I feel a deep, secret loneliness? Why is it that I have a Ph.D. in clinical psychology and a master of divinity and work as a pastor and yet I'm not sure who I am?[18]

He is not alone in needing to ask such important questions as a pastor. From my own years of church involvement, I have come to the conclusion that all those in leadership roles need to work hard at discovering who they are before ever becoming responsible for the care of others in the Body of Christ. In training for ministry, we can gain all sorts of knowledge about God and the Scriptures, about how to reach out to others and about how to 'do' church in general. But unless

---

18   John Ortberg *Soul Keeping* Zondervan 2014 p 23

we also gain more self-understanding, we may well find ourselves caught in some desolate space between our public and private persona, always feeling a little restless and unfulfilled, shutting our true self off somewhere within us rather than living out our faith in an authentic manner. This, in turn, can affect our ability to pastor and lead others in the most helpful way possible and also to relate with our colleagues in ministry in a healthy way.

Yet, whatever our role or career, it is so important to know ourselves and live in the light of that knowledge. Yes, it may involve putting aside time in the midst of our busy schedules to reflect, to be still and to let God, who knows everything about us, tell us who we are. And it may take considerable effort—and courage at times—to delve deeper within ourselves and come to grips with what we find. Yet, through it all, we know God's Spirit will be with us and in us to comfort, encourage and inspire. In fact, only in God, I would be bold enough to say, can we have the deep security we most need to embark on such an undertaking—that security that comes from knowing our Creator God loves us perfectly, accepts us unconditionally and forgives us totally. How blessed we are, as people of faith, to be able to set out on such a journey of discovery, knowing our great, compassionate God is walking with us and cheering us on each step of the way!

For reflection

- Do you find it hard to give yourself permission to rest? If so, why do you think this is the case? What things could you change in your life to enable you to find that time to be rather than do?

- In Philippians 3, the Apostle Paul, after reflecting on his past journey, talks about forgetting what is behind and pressing on towards what lies ahead. Do you struggle at times to put aside what has happened in the past and focus on what you can do now that will enrich your life and the lives of others? If so, take a few moments to be quiet, recognise the Holy Spirit's presence, empowering and comfort in you and around you, and hand these past issues or failures over to God.

- *'Know thyself'* is an Ancient Greek saying, often attributed to Socrates. How important do you think it is for us to know ourselves as best we can? Do you feel our lack of self-understanding can hamper us in relating to and caring for others? In what ways?

- Is it time for you to make space for God in a more intentional way in your life? Is it time for you to step aside from some commitments that are draining you and allow God to help you find or regain that sense of who you are? Is there someone you know who could accompany you on this journey? Ask God to show you the next step and to provide whatever resources you need for your own experience of delving deeper into God and into who you are.

Chapter Eleven
Letting That Creativity Loose

The Lord directs the steps of the godly. He delights in every detail of their lives. Though they stumble, they will never fall, for the Lord holds them by the hand. Psalm 37:23-24 NLT

The very steps we take come from God; otherwise how would we know where we're going? Proverbs 20:24 The Message

It seems to me we often know deep down what the next step God has for us in our lives might be, well before we are prepared to admit it or consider taking it. Sometimes it is as if an unseen hand is drawing us along a particular path that appears interesting and even exciting, yet we feel so inadequate and ill-equipped to step out and do what we sense we are being called to do. We try to resist, determined to choose our own way. But, in the end, we find this pull on our lives too strong and are dragged, sometimes almost kicking and screaming, towards what lies ahead.

This may happen to us in different areas of our lives—in our choice of career, in our relationships or even in our faith journey. C S Lewis, for example, found himself in this situation when confronted with God, the 'I am', in a way that horrified him but left him with little alternative:

You must picture me alone in that room at Magdalen, night after night, feeling, whenever my mind lifted even for a second from my work, the steady, unrelenting approach of Him whom I so earnestly desired not to meet. That which I greatly feared had at last come upon me. In the Trinity Term of 1929 I gave in, and admitted that God was God, and knelt and prayed: perhaps, that night, the most dejected and reluctant convert in all England.[19]

Lewis goes on to describe how he did not appreciate until later the amazing humility and mercy of God that would accept such a reluctant, resentful prodigal and persevere in drawing him towards belief and, ultimately, to freedom:

The hardness of God is kinder than the softness of men, and His compulsion is our liberation.[20]

My journey to faith in God was, of course, nothing like C S Lewis's. Yet, without understanding it, I too had felt that kind but compelling call of God in my life prior to my conversion in several ways—the attractive words of that children's evangelist in the little gospel chapel near our home; the hope expressed in those hymns at my headmaster's funeral; the hush of holiness in the old Anglican church where I was confirmed; the sense of rightness in those Scripture verses I heard over the years and came to love. I had also felt God's firm, guiding hand in choosing my life partner that day outside the old, wooden church in Brisbane, as I watched Lionel greet people at the door. At that moment, with a sense of inevitability and even a touch of resentment that my future had been made so clear, I knew he was the person I was meant to marry. Now, in a somewhat similar way, I felt God drawing me with determination along that rocky road towards becoming a writer.

From my early years, I had loved writing. For me, it was no great chore to labour over those primary school compositions and the creative writing essays that followed at high school. At university,

19	C S Lewis *Surprised by Joy* Fontana Books 1959 p 182
20	Ibid p 183

there was little opportunity for creativity in the foreign language and history subjects I studied—or even, strange to say, in the one English unit I took. Yet that love of writing must have stayed with me because, somewhere in my early years of marriage, I am told I wrote an update about myself for our high school alumni newsletter that mentioned my dream of writing a book one day. After we moved interstate and our family grew, that dream receded, as I immersed myself in motherhood and focussed more on music and church activities. Yet I well remember the hours I spent during those years writing long letters to my parents back home in Queensland and to other family members.

Each week without fail, my mother would write to me. And each week, I would be expected to write back, yet never in any brief, careless way. My letters home were always long, wordy epistles—four or five pages of cramped, almost illegible handwriting which often spilled over onto the back of the large sheets of writing paper I used. They were by no means literary masterpieces, filled as they were with snippets of information about our children's most recent accomplishments or mundane details about gardening or cooking or sewing. Yet I can remember the satisfaction I felt as I wrote them, despite the time it took to do so. After the children were asleep, I would curl up in front of our open fire during the long, South Australian winters and write to my heart's content, stopping every so often to gaze into the flames and reflect. I loved the whole experience of composing something that would, I hoped, bring joy to the person who read it. I delighted in painting vivid word-pictures of our family life and activities and in describing the beautiful area where we lived. Although I was unaware of it, I suspect God was even then nurturing that creative streak in me that expressed itself best in writing.

After we moved back to Sydney, we were privileged to have a brave, Czech woman in our church whose story touched and inspired me.

'How is she still standing, after everything that has happened to her in her life?' I would ask Lionel. 'One day, I'm going to write a book about her.'

Yet, in my heart, I never thought I would. It was too far-fetched and wonderful a dream even to contemplate. As our children grew up, I tried my hand at poetry and a few short stories, but little came of it. Instead, I returned to study and to work, then to study for a second time, followed by ministry, all of which removed any thoughts of writing even further from my mind. Yet the dream did not leave me entirely, because at one stage in my final months on our ministry team, I remember sharing in a women's group I led how I had ideas for five novels in my head. This desire to write continued to strengthen until, on the evening of my church farewell, I told everyone present that, in the coming months, I hoped to begin writing a book.

Somewhere within me then, this urge to write had lain hidden, stirring slightly and making its presence felt from time to time, but waiting for that moment when I was ready, willing and able to pay attention to it. Now, halfway through my sabbatical year, it seemed that moment was edging closer. My heart leapt at the idea. Yet those layers of self-doubt and self-protection also began to work overtime. I did not know enough about writing, I reasoned. There were too many other important things waiting to be done, once I had rested a little more. Besides, what if, after spending months writing a book, no one wanted to publish it? What if it turned out to be terrible? Anyway, why add to that almost overwhelming mountain of books already available in Christian bookstores?

In June 2003, I travelled overseas to visit a friend living and working in Turkey. And it was there God challenged me in no uncertain terms to come home and start writing. As I read from the Book of Isaiah one morning, I realised God was showing me I had closed my ears to this inner call to write for long enough. I now needed to pay attention to what I was hearing, seize the moment and act. It was as if God had become almost weary of my many excuses and was urging me in a way even I could not ignore to let go of those layers that hid my true self and allow the writer inside to emerge.

As soon as I came home, I applied myself to learning more about writing and the world of publishing. Now I was determined to step out and do what I felt God had called me to do. I started planning out my first novel, a story inspired by the Czech lady I had met years earlier, now sadly no longer alive, and began to write my introductory chapters. Yet I was still plagued with self-doubt about it all. Who was I to think I could write a novel anyone else would want to read? How would I ever be able to make it to the ninety thousand or more words required for a full-length novel?

In order to gain more confidence to write what was stirring inside me, I decided to attend some seminars for emerging writers at the New South Wales Writers' Centre. While these provided me with much needed information and a realistic glimpse into the world of publication, they also had a marked negative impact on me. At times, I would come away feeling the whole idea of writing anything worthy of being published was even crazier than I had thought. It was all too hard. If the authors I heard speak had needed to struggle for so long to find a publisher and then to promote their books, what chance did I have of succeeding? These seminars were intended to encourage and empower would-be authors, but for someone like me so filled with self-doubt, they often had the opposite effect. Later in my writing journey, I benefited in a significant way from other courses and events at the Writers' Centre. But at that point, my dream was a little too fragile, as was I, to take on board too much of what I heard.

I also found it hard to remain positive when well-meaning friends and acquaintances enquired about how I now filled my days.

'We know you're writing a book, but ... well, what do you do?'

'They have no idea how much work is involved in writing a novel!' I would fume later to anyone who would listen. 'It's so obvious they don't believe I can do it. Besides, I get the strong impression they don't think writing is a legitimate thing for me to be doing anyway, compared with "real ministry"!'

I suspect my own doubts about my writing and its value often distorted the true intent of such questions. Nevertheless, they managed to stir up even more uncertainty in me. On the other hand, I treasured those friends who cheered me on and were delighted to see me following a dream I had harboured for so long. My family, who had put up for years with listening to my ideas about the book I would write 'one day', supported me every step of the way. And my patient soul friend Joy continued to believe in me through all the twists and turns of my writing journey. One of the greatest gifts we can give others, in my opinion, is the gift of believing in them and of seeing the potential God has put in them, even when they do not see it or believe in it themselves.

Little by little, as I allowed myself to become caught up in my writing, I realised something significant was beginning to happen deep inside. In many ways, it was reminiscent of an experience I had had not long before I left our church. During a counselling session, the art therapist I was seeing at the time invited me to use paint and crayons to express my feelings about leaving. I had never studied art at school and knew I was no artist. Yet the sense of release I experienced, as I spread that purple paint across my blank sheet of paper with such deep, raw emotion, was almost shocking in its intensity. Now, as I began to let the words flow with more and more freedom, I could sense something of that same release taking place. It was exciting, but also a little intimidating.

What would happen if I allowed all those ideas inside me to bubble up to the surface and be exposed in print for everyone to see? What would people think?

It was not long before I also began to experience the strong sense of isolation that can be part and parcel of being a writer. I could attend all sorts of writing workshops and seminars. I could join a writers' group and share my work with peers on the same journey. But, in the end, I needed to sit down and write my own book—no one else could do that for me. Others might give me advice and feedback, but it was up to me to press on, alone. And that brought with it a responsibility I did not want at first and one I feared I was inadequate to shoulder.

At the same time, I knew I was not alone. I was well aware God was with me each day as I opened my laptop. In those first weeks and months when I had little idea what I was doing, I would sometimes pray out loud, asking God all those desperate questions that lurked inside me. *Is this how you write, Lord? Is this the direction you want my story to take?* In the moments that followed, I would often feel God's Spirit flooding my mind and body, reassuring me I was on the right path and strengthening me to keep going.

I soon came to realise, however, that this journey with God into those unexplored, creative parts of me was about something more than producing a book. God was interested in the whole of me and did not intend to leave that self-doubt of mine alone.

'Sometimes I think God has such a great sense of humour!' I commented to a friend one day. 'Of all the things I could have ended up doing, God leads me into writing. This must be one of the biggest challenges possible for someone struggling with self-doubt!'

Up to that point, I had not been prepared to share those early chapters of my first draft with anyone. The risk of rejection was far too great. Yet at times, I pictured God smiling at me as I wrote and saying in a gentle voice:

It's all right, Jo-Anne. I'm here. I know this is a big step for you, but keep going! And remember, whether you write another word or not, I will love you just the same.

I knew God was trying to show me that I had permission to succeed or fail, to write or not to write. It did not matter as far as our relationship was concerned. In my loving and gracious God, I had a safe haven—that place where I could be me and where any mistakes I made or failures I experienced would not destroy me. And the strong sense of security that gave me as I stepped out on my writing journey was wonderful. Even though my legs were a little shaky and even though I was aware there would be times of great testing ahead, I knew that the firm foundation the Lord gave King David would always be there for me too:

I waited patiently for the Lord; he turned to me and heard my cry, he lifted me out of the slimy pit, out of the mud and mire; he set my feet on a rock and gave me a firm place to stand. Psalm 40:1-2

As the months passed, I began to feel I was well on the way to reinventing myself and becoming the rest of what I was able to be, as Joan Chittister puts it in her book *Scarred by Struggle, Transformed by Hope*.[21] Or perhaps it was more that God was doing this reinventing within me, as I gave myself over to the whole creative process of breathing life into something that had lain dormant inside me for so long. As the words flowed and my story unfolded, the sheer joy and fulfilment I experienced amazed me. At times, I felt as if I was being carried along on some river of creativity that originated in the very heart of our Creator God.

Then I began to notice something else surprising. It was as if a switch had been turned on inside me so that my eyes were opened and I was able to see God's incredible, vibrant creativity all around me in a way I had never experienced before. Words almost failed me whenever I tried to explain this to others.

'When I look out at our garden, it's ... well, it's as if the trees and shrubs are greener! I seem to see them in 3D—they somehow stand out more and look so alive. And there are so many different colours and shapes and textures everywhere too. It's amazing!'

In turn, this fresh experience of seeing God's glorious handiwork in nature seemed to stir up more creativity in me in a way that was also hard to describe. In my first months of writing, I would often drive to nearby Lake Parramatta and gaze at the trees, noticing the gentle

---

21   Joan Chittister *Scarred by Struggle, Transformed by Hope* William B Eerdmans 2003 p 63

movement of their leaves in the breeze, or watch the ripples on the surface of the lake as the ducks took to flight. Sometimes, I would also marvel at the minute and intricate extravagancies of nature to be seen in the nearby bushland—the creativity displayed in one exquisite, tiny wildflower or one microscopic insect that seemed so insignificant in the big scheme of things.

Something within me was coming alive. And I knew God was such an integral part of it all.

As my novel began to take shape, I came to enjoy the unique challenge of creating another whole world and to revel in bringing my characters to life. At times, I felt as if I was pouring myself into their hearts and lives, identifying with all their emotions and experiences, willing them on to succeed in every endeavour. My first novel was a sad story, yet one also filled with hope, as the main character, Heléna, holds onto her faith in God through all the catastrophes she faces in life. I had never experienced anything like the challenges I was writing about. Yet, somehow, the whole process of expressing my character's grief and helping her work through her terrible losses became a cathartic journey for me as well. As I realised what was happening, I marvelled at the grace of God in leading me to write a story that would bring me so much vicarious healing, along with so much personal fulfilment.

By the end of 2004, after over a year of writing, the first draft of my novel *Heléna* was complete. I could not believe I had managed to craft a story that seemed to flow in a way I felt was right and that conveyed all I wanted to convey. I had wondered if I would make it to ninety thousand words but ended up with almost twice that—far too many for a debut novel, as I later discovered when seeking out a potential publisher. But first of all, my precious work needed much pruning and editing. I cringed at the thought of the pain involved in letting others read something almost sacred to me, yet I knew it was necessary. Author and pastor Mandy Smith has expressed well how I felt:

> *You step into a creative process that is sometimes cruel and raw, a little too close for comfort. Then, with shaking hands, you put that outpouring of your soul into a public form and hope that someone understands.*[22]

I was unsure I was ready for such exposure, even within that small circle of family and friends to whom I planned to entrust my precious first draft. Yet I had invested so much of myself in my novel and I wanted to see it published. Besides, by then, I was too far down the road of self-discovery as well to want to turn around and opt out of the whole experience.

Those early manuscript readers were kind, but also honest and thorough. I valued all their comments, although, in my insecure state, I tried at first to take too many of these on board. I wanted to honour all the work my friends had put in on my behalf, yet it was impossible to act on each and every one of their suggestions. I was torn—and soon realised how much I still hated having anyone regard me in a negative light. In the end, this experience taught me much about taking constructive criticism on board but also about being prepared to risk displeasing others, in order to stay true to what I wanted to write. I needed to listen to my manuscript readers, yet not allow their voices to drown out my own creative voice that was clamouring so hard to be heard.

In the months that followed, I decided to test the waters and contact several potential publishers. I sent off the first chapters of my manuscript to one large publishing house far too soon, only, of course, to have it rejected. I decided to enter these same chapters in a well-known literary competition, hoping this would provide a quick path to publication. I did not come anywhere near winning, although I did receive some helpful feedback. As time went on and other rejections followed, I became more realistic in approaching those few publishers willing to accept unsolicited manuscripts from first-time authors. And,

---

[22] Mandy Smith 'Experts in Weakness' in Leadership Journal April 2014

while waiting for their responses, I decided to try my hand at entering some short story competitions. Writing short stories was not where my heart lay, but I felt the discipline of having to stick to the various word limits required might help me refine my writing and editing skills. I believe this proved true, although my general lack of success in these competitions did nothing to boost my confidence in being an author.

As I wrote, I also wanted to keep on discovering more of my creative self and soon found Julia Cameron's book *The Artist's Way*[23] so helpful in this regard. Having tasted the joy of getting to know that creative person inside me, I did not want to abandon her again, as Julia Cameron suggests we often do to that part of us we find hard to embrace.[24] Therefore, whether or not I was able to find a publisher for my first novel, I knew the time had come for me to throw myself into writing my next and to endeavour to bring a whole new set of characters to life. I had several possible story outlines in mind but, in the end, chose to proceed with writing *Laura*, a story inspired by my friend who had become blind as a child. In this novel, I planned to focus on the theme of receiving God's love and of allowing God to tell us who we are—themes close to my heart at that point in my journey. I wanted to write with integrity out of my own experience and, in the process, share what I felt was a powerful story in a way that would make a real difference in the lives of my readers.

Then, one day towards the end of 2005, I opened my laptop to find an email from a publisher I had contacted months earlier. It began:

We would like to inform you that we are interested in publishing your novel Heléna.

Because of the long period that had elapsed since submitting my manuscript to this particular publisher, I had decided to discount them. Now I could not believe what I was reading. After the initial shock wore off, however, I gathered my wits and checked out their offer further. It seemed reasonable and, in the end, I accepted it with a thankful heart. I

---

23   Julia Cameron *The Artist's Way: A Spiritual Path to Higher Creativity* Pan 1992
24   Ibid p 98

was now about to embark on another whole new and scary part of my journey—that of publication.

For several months, I heard nothing more from this publisher. Then, just when I had begun to wonder what was happening, I received another email from them:

We feel your novel is too long to publish as it is, especially for a first-time author. Would you consider dividing it into two?

My heart sank. How could I ever do such a thing? I did not even want to contemplate tackling what seemed to me an impossible task. At first, I put off making any decision about it, because my mind was elsewhere. By this time, my new novel *Laura* had also struck some difficulties. I had sent the first few chapters to my friend who had inspired me to write this story and had received some strong criticism from her regarding various assumptions I had made about growing up with vision impairment.

I am thankful that, with time and perseverance, along with much fervent prayer, both these situations were resolved in a positive way. I managed to rework the first two-thirds of my original *Heléna* manuscript and thus create a shorter novel of the same name. I put the remaining third aside, to be expanded at a later date to create a second novel of similar length, *All the Days of My Life*. And I was also able to rewrite those sections of *Laura* that needed changing and to liaise further with my friend about the misinformation I had included. As a result of dealing with both these challenges, I believe I grew as a person and an author, although not without cost.

I was fast learning to be prepared to be challenged and stretched at every level, if I wanted to become the writer I believed I was created to be. I had chosen an interesting road on which to travel, with so many unique twists and turns, but I knew I had made the right choice. In a sense, it had been made for me, long before I realised it. In a strange, almost surreal way, I felt I was once again that little girl who had loved to read and dream and write her school compositions so many years earlier. Those protective inner layers of mine were being removed at a rapid rate, as my writing journey unfolded, allowing that little girl within to poke her head out and be seen. Sometimes, I still felt like hiding under those layers again, just as I had done beneath the bedclothes as a child, and curling up with my thumb in my mouth. But, for the most part, I was excited to step out and face the future, secure in the knowledge that God would guide and watch over me.

Now I was beginning to realise who I was. Now I was beginning to hear, loud and clear, the simple but profound challenge given by Rob Bell in his book *Velvet Elvis* and to respond to it:

Somewhere in you is the you whom you were made to be. We need you to be you. We don't need a second anybody. We need the first you.[25]

For reflection

- Sometimes early on in our lives, God seems to give us a glimpse of the person we were created to be, although we do not come to understand it fully until much later. Have you found this to be true in your own life? Where do you feel you are right now in being the person God created you to be?

- How strong do you feel the connection is between what we want to do and be in our heart of hearts and what God is calling us to do? What has your experience been in this regard?

- Have you ever had others criticise something you have created and worked hard to produce? How did you handle it? Were you able to deal with it in God's strength and move on or was it a devastating experience for you?

- Read again the words of Psalm 37:23-24 at the beginning of this chapter. In your life, how have you experienced the Lord directing your steps and holding you so you did not fall?

---

25   Rob Bell *Velvet Elvis* Zondervan 2005 p 150

Perhaps right now, you are about to step out into some creative venture of your own or are dealing with some other change in your life. If so, reflect on these verses again and ask the Lord to pour his strength and peace into your heart, as you face whatever lies ahead.

Chapter Twelve

Staying Real

"You are the light of the world—like a city on a hilltop that cannot be hidden. No one lights a lamp and then puts it under a basket. Instead, a lamp is placed on a stand, where it gives light to everyone in the house. In the same way, let your good deeds shine out for all to see, so that everyone will praise your heavenly Father. Matthew 5:14-16 NLT

I find it wonderful that God is willing and able to give us a glimpse of what lies ahead on those occasions when this knowledge will help us in some way. I am grateful God made it clear to me, for example, via that still, small voice in my spirit, that one day I would be part of the ministry team at our church, because this enabled me to begin to prepare myself for this possible outcome. But I am equally grateful I did not know ahead of time how difficult those years of study at theological college would turn out to be. Otherwise, I might never have found the courage to tackle them. I am also thankful for the clear call I heard while in Turkey to come home and start writing, because this left no room for any doubt as to what God wanted me to do. But I am equally thankful God showed me only that initial step in my writing journey and no more. Otherwise, I might have hesitated to begin at all, had I known then what being a published author would entail.

Writing my first novel was, without doubt, an amazing, fulfilling, cathartic experience. I changed a great deal in the process and became much more of the person I believe God created me to be. Many of my friends saw the difference writing made in my life and, although they might not have understood how this happened, they were delighted for me. I knew I was more at peace within myself. I felt more alive than I had for a long while. And, in a way that is difficult to describe, my whole life seemed somehow more authentic and real. I was free to be me—I did not have to please a boss or be answerable to any employer other than God. I had no real deadlines to meet and could write whatever God put on my heart to write, without being too concerned about the opinions of others.

Once my novel was accepted for publication and I had signed that contract, however, the picture began to change. Early in 2007, as the release date for *Heléna* drew near, I was filled with a mixture of excitement and trepidation. Publication means just that—the act of making something public or known. Now my own work, which had hitherto been read by a mere handful of people, was about to become available to anyone and everyone. A few months earlier at a writers' event, someone had asked me what I had thought was a strange question at the time:

'But ... do you really want to be published?'

I mumbled some sort of response, but my mind was whirling. Why would a writer not aim to be published? Why would anyone spend weeks, months, even years writing something, yet not want others to read it? To me, that seemed crazy.

Later, I began to realise what might have prompted this man's question. Perhaps, for him, the mere process of expressing his inner thoughts was fulfilment enough—and I could understand that. After all, I too had experienced the cathartic nature of writing. Or perhaps he could not face the thought of having his precious words torn to shreds—and I could understand that as well. I had struggled with sharing my manuscript even with that small group of people willing to critique it and had taken each comment to heart. Why would I want to put myself through the torture of having others who might be less kind and constructive read my work?

Yet I wanted my novel out there. Just as we welcome the arrival of a human baby, I hoped others would rejoice with me that my literary baby had at last entered the world and would love her as well. At the same time, I knew I needed to be humble and realistic. After all, this was my first novel—and I had attended enough writers' seminars to know there were bound to be many flaws in it. But beyond that, I wanted God to be honoured through what I had written. I hoped my readers would enjoy the story itself. But I also hoped some at least would engage with the timeless truths about God I had woven into it—in particular, the concept of holding onto our faith in God, whatever happens in life. I wanted God to touch their hearts and bring them deep comfort and encouragement. But how could this happen, if I did not see my book through to publication?

I remember well the moment I saw the proposed cover of *Heléna* for the first time. My laptop was open on our kitchen table and, since it was late in the day, I was alternating between writing and preparing dinner. While checking my emails, I found one from my publisher and opened the attached image. And there, filling the whole screen in an instant, was my cover. The scene featured on it—a narrow, cobbled street in the old section of a European city—seemed to draw me in and captured the mood of the book well. I gasped in delight—I loved it so much. Then, with a sense of shock, I saw my name in capital letters above that image and again down the spine. And there too was my photo and author bio on the back cover.

At that point, I recalled the question the man at the Writers' Centre had asked about whether I truly wanted to be published. Now I had a different question of my own.

'What have I *done*?'

I felt so vulnerable and exposed. Now I had to own every word inside that beautiful cover. What would people think? Even more to the point, what would my friends and those whose opinions I valued the most think? I could not back out now, but I was shocked at what I had done.

As the date of my book launch approached, I began to empathise much more with artists who set out to display their precious paintings for the first time in some obscure gallery or composers who, with trembling fingers, share some new work with a perhaps unappreciative audience. I comforted myself with the thought that, as an author, at least I would be spared those immediate, gut-level responses they had to endure. Anyone who purchased my novel would need to read it first, before passing judgement on anything other than the cover or the size of the book or the font chosen. They might not get to read it for some time either. And they might also be kind enough to remain silent, if they hated it.

There I was, still replaying the question that had taken root in my mind all those years earlier—'But what would people think?' There I was, still falling back into old ways of responding that I knew were quite childish. I remembered then the words of Paul in that regard:

When I was a child, I spoke and thought and reasoned as a child does. But when I grew up, I put away childish things.
1 Corinthians 13:11 NLT

There was no choice but to face whatever lay ahead. I had known that becoming a published author was destined to attack my self-doubt and desire for self-protection in a huge and ongoing way. That was the reality of the situation, so I needed to get used to it and grow up. Yet, even at that point, I sensed God's heart was to care for all of me, including that vulnerable little girl still hiding somewhere inside—that kernel of my true self still learning to open up to the world. Again, I pictured God smiling at me and reassuring me in such a gentle, loving voice.

Don't worry, Jo-Anne. This is the best way forward for you. Just enjoy the ride! I will be with you through it all.

In the end, I was delighted with the warm reception *Heléna* received. Not everyone loved it, of course. Some found my main character too good to be true. Some found my writing far too wordy. Some found my style too stilted and the dialogue too unrealistic. But others told me they had had trouble putting my book down, which encouraged me so much. I soon realised that, if I took every comment and review I received to heart, I would find myself flung back and forth on a wild roller-coaster of emotions, at the mercy of the opinions of others. I needed to learn to give such critiques over to God for safe keeping until I could consider them in a more measured way and decide what to take on board and what to let drift away. And, as other published authors had warned me, I needed to develop the hide of an elephant, while still maintaining that sensitive writer's heart.

Not long after *Heléna* was released in 2007, I began another whole journey—that of speaking in public again. One aspect of local church ministry I had missed most was the opportunity to speak in services and at other meetings. Now I was overwhelmed that God had not only given me my heart's desire to write my first published novel but was also restoring to me a ministry I loved. In his book *Soul Survivor*, Philip Yancey, after visiting the American pastor and author Frederick Buechner, writes the following:

Not a single other dwelling is visible from Buechner's study: leaning on an invisible pulpit, he addresses an invisible audience.[26]

I found I was able to relate easily to this image of leaning on an invisible pulpit. It described so well how I too felt at times, writing by myself at my laptop with my own invisible audience in mind. Now I sensed God smiling at me, almost with a conspiratorial wink, and offering me a new yet familiar challenge.

Come on, Jo-Anne—time to start speaking again!

I decided to grasp every opportunity to speak that came my way. I

---

26   Philip Yancey *Soul Survivor* Hodder and Stoughton 2001 p 253

was eager to see what God might do through this new style of ministry I had been given which seemed such a perfect fit for me. Whenever I stood up to address an audience, I felt as if every part of me coalesced in that moment, as if my God-given gifts and personality and all my life experiences blended together, enabling me to share from the heart with joy and conviction. I felt fulfilled and whole—and so blessed. I believed I had indeed found that special place Frederick Buechner himself describes so well:

The place God calls you to is the place where your deep gladness and the world's deep hunger meet.[27]

In the years that followed, further opportunities to speak emerged as more of my novels were published in quick succession—*All the Days of My Life* (2008), *Laura* (2009), *Jenna* (2010) and *Heléna's Legacy* (2011). Then, after changing publishers, my first memoir, *Soul Friend*, was released in 2012, followed by another novel, *The Inheritance*, in 2013. During these years, I often spoke to church groups on the various themes highlighted in my books—holding onto our faith in God, receiving God's love, using our God-given gifts, forgiveness, the value of spiritual friendships. At more secular venues, I shared about the road to publication, as well as about my own writing journey. I was very grateful when someone who had heard me before would recommend me to another group as a speaker, but I soon learnt I needed to step out and find these speaking engagements myself as well. I knew I had been given some ability to network and realised I now needed to use this to seek out new places to speak, as God led. But God also often surprised me by connecting me with people and groups in ways I could never have envisaged.

In some years, speaking commitments and promotional opportunities came thick and fast. During interstate trips, I would of course schedule as many of these as I could, in order to make good use of my time away. But even when home, these engagements would

---

[27] Frederick Buechner *Listening to Your Life* HarperCollins 1992 p 186

sometimes end up close together, almost making my head spin. I enjoyed it all, but it was not always good for me. Along the way, I came to realise how easy it would be, in the midst of so much activity, to lose sight of that true self I was beginning to discover through my writing.

At times, we become too busy because of factors beyond our control. Our boss asks us to work longer hours. We are studying and have assignments due. Our children need us to take them to various extra-curricular activities. Other family responsibilities crop up. But even if we have personal control of our own workload, as I did, we can soon manage to become overcommitted. We might have the best intentions of not taking on too much, of leaving space for God in our lives, of spending more time with family and friends, of enjoying some creative or leisure activity. Yet we are so often tempted to let those good intentions go by the board and so reluctant at times to say no to adding yet another event to our already busy schedules.

This was a temptation I could not always resist. In the midst of it all, I tried to continue writing, but it was often difficult, after speaking somewhere, to get back into my writer's head and pick up my train of thought where I had left off. I knew I needed long periods of uninterrupted quietness to help me tap into that creative part of me, become aware again of God's presence around me and produce writing that was satisfying and authentic. Yet, like many other authors, I struggled at times to safeguard those creative spaces. Former publisher Allen Arnold has described this dilemma well:

> *We get so busy doing that we can forget how to be still and approach our art as holy ground. Maybe that's why some Christian speakers, books, and conferences end up focusing almost all of their time teaching writers about craft and how to get published – and so little time on how to actually create with God.*[28]

It was true I needed this quality writing time to stay true to the real me and to be able to express God's heart through my writing.

---

[28] Allen Arnold in 'Novel Rocket' blog 20 June 2014

But I also needed it in order to maintain my general wellbeing. As an introvert, I find myself drained rather than energised by too much contact with people. Of course, writing can also become exhausting when our ideas do not seem to flow or when we are at the often painful editing and revision stage. But my busy speaking schedule and the constant relating to diverse groups of people produced a different set of challenges. I enjoyed preparing and delivering the things God put on my heart to share wherever I spoke. I loved being part of what God was doing in people's lives in this way. But I also needed time alone afterwards to re-group and replenish that emotional tank inside me that seemed to drain out at an alarming rate during these times.

For me, writing provided that life-giving space I needed where I could again become immersed in the creative process and, in turn, be re-created myself. I therefore had to allow myself to say no on occasions, even to family commitments or catch-ups with friends, in order to guard this time alone. But I also began to realise I needed to give myself permission to feed my spirit in other ways I loved—seeing beautiful things, listening to music, playing the piano, reading, doing nothing.

One day, I attended a meeting of Christian women leaders in a beautiful home overlooking one of Sydney's most popular beaches. After the meeting, I wandered around one of several large sitting rooms in this home, drinking in the beauty of the ocean views outside and gazing in awe at the exquisite works of art on display inside. On almost every wall, I saw stunning, original paintings by famous artists. And in the centre of the room stood a grand piano, its lid up, as if inviting someone to sit down and play.

I gazed at it all for some time, allowing the rich beauty around me to feed my spirit. Later, as I tried to thank our hostess for sharing her wonderful home with us, the tears welled up.

'I ... I can't tell you how much being here has meant to me. It's all so beautiful. It's such a gift to a writer to see things like this ...'

I could not go any further, but she nodded and seemed to understand. And, as I glanced around me one more time before leaving, I sensed God smiling at me, delighted to bless and refresh me in such a special way.

Above all, however, the most serious challenge I faced as a result of my too-busy speaking schedule was that of maintaining my close, life-giving relationship with God. I knew I had to safeguard those times of quiet, listening prayer to understand what God wanted me to say wherever I spoke and also to be able to speak with integrity. In *Immortal Diamond*, Richard Rohr states:

The True Self is a shared and sharable self, or it is not the True Self.[29]

I needed those times with God so I could remember who I was and keep allowing the real me God had created to shine through. I wanted to speak with transparency from my true 'shared and sharable' self—I did not want to pretend to be other than I was. And I knew that, without the power and insight God's Spirit can give, I would be no more than an empty vessel, saying many words yet unable to provide that life-giving water we all need.

Why did I allow myself to become so busy, given how unhelpful it was on various levels? I believed all my speaking engagements were opportunities from God. Yet I also wondered if my old desire to please everyone and my hatred of saying no made me over-eager at times to fall in with others' plans and ignore my own needs. That little girl within was still learning to stand tall in her own right and still did not want to disappoint others or cause them to think less of her in any way. I needed to learn to hear God's clear 'yes' before committing myself as often as I did. And I also needed to remember that my sense of security was to be found first and foremost in God and not in the opinions of others. I could decline with grace when necessary and the sky would not fall in.

Did I also perhaps feel some inward pressure to speak as much

---

29   Richard Rohr op cit p 160

as I did in order to justify the long hours spent writing? I believed my books could make a difference in others' lives, but speaking was a much more direct way of ministering to people. Memories of those old comments some people had made when I first began writing still surfaced at times.

'We know you're writing, but what else do you do?'

'We know you're not in ministry anymore and that's a shame. What are you doing?'

I still needed to take far less notice of what others thought about my choosing to write and, instead, focus on doing what God had called and gifted me to do, being true to myself in the process.

Besides over-committing myself, another trap I encountered in my speaking journey was my tendency to hold a lengthy post mortem after each engagement. I soon discovered how expert I was at losing perspective and remembering only the worst parts of my input, especially when tired. At times, this even gave rise to those old feelings of embarrassment and shame I thought God had dealt with years earlier. I knew it was up to me to refuse to take these on board again and instead, to live in the reality of God's complete love and acceptance. I always believed it was important, after speaking somewhere, to reflect on what parts seemed to connect well with my audience and what parts had felt laboured. I wanted to learn any lessons God had for me along the way and to realise when I had perhaps said things I thought were clever or insightful but were not what God had wanted me to say. But I also needed to stop beating myself up over my mistakes. Just as the Apostle Paul talks about in Philippians 3:13-14, I had to learn to put it all behind me and press on, straining towards what lay ahead rather than dwelling on the past.

To me, this was all part and parcel of acknowledging that self-doubting, perfectionist little girl inside who clamoured to be heard on occasions, reassuring her she could trust God to be her refuge and protector and move on, with her head held high. I saw her as my true self in childlike form—that intrinsic part of me created in the image of God who needed to be nurtured and allowed to grow and develop into full maturity. And I knew I needed to take time to listen to and befriend this core part of me within, as psychologist David Benner maintains:

We must befriend the self we seek to know. We must befriend it with hospitality, not hostility.[30]

Only then would I be able to become all God had created me to be. Only then would I be able to come home to my true self and be comfortable in who I was.

With both my speaking and writing, a further issue I had to face was what financial return might or might not result from all my efforts. I knew that, in Australia at least, writing novels with strong Christian themes was not the way to amass a fortune. Did I then have the right to spend so much time and energy on a pursuit that would, in all likelihood, provide little monetary reward? Early on in my writing journey, a wise Christian friend tried to help me gain a better perspective on this.

'I've wanted to write a novel for a long time,' I told him one day, my voice somewhat defensive. 'I hope it might be a way to make some extra money so I can support my friend in Turkey more.'

'Well, that's fine—if you need that as an excuse to write,' he responded in his gentle but challenging way.

At first, I was shocked. Was he saying I was lying about wanting to support my friend more? As I thought about it, however, I realised he was trying to give me a precious gift. He was encouraging me to forget about the whole matter of money and to allow myself to do what I wanted to do and what God had also called and gifted me to do with all my heart.

It was indeed enough for me to write for the joy and fulfilment it brought and in the expectation that my words would bless and encourage others, irrespective of any financial return. And I wanted to stay real and true to myself in the process, writing what I believed

---

30   David Benner *The Gift of Being Yourself* IVP 2004 p 57

God wanted me to write rather than what might sell better in the current market. Yet I also hoped I could make some small profit from book sales and royalties—or at least not cause any significant drain on our own limited resources. Even having a traditional publisher, I still needed to purchase my own stock, if I wished to sell my books wherever I spoke. It therefore made good business sense to ensure these costs were recouped within a reasonable timeframe. Yet, despite that, I wanted God to be the driving force behind my whole writing journey, not money.

As far as any financial return from speaking engagements was concerned, from the beginning, I chose not to charge a speaker's fee. At times, I was grateful to receive a monetary gift to help defray travel costs, but I preferred to leave each group free to decide for themselves what they could afford. Yet, in doing so, I was aware I was walking something of a tightrope. As family members pointed out, a secular speaker would charge a hefty fee for giving a writing workshop or taking the equivalent of a weekend retreat. Did I not value myself enough to charge something at least? Had I forgotten Jesus' words in Luke 10:7 about workers being worth their wage? I heard what they were saying, but still could not bring myself to charge. I am sure this was partly because I still did not value myself and the gifts God had given me enough, yet I did not want to cut out smaller groups who might be unable to afford anything at all. In every situation, I wanted to be able to speak with authenticity from a generous heart and not for any mercenary reason.

I also faced a different challenge in my quest to stay real when I was invited to speak at service clubs and other community groups. I was happy to talk about my writing journey and about the challenges and joys of being published, but sometimes, my old desire for everyone to approve of me prevented me from mentioning my faith in God as much as I sensed I could and should in these settings. As time went on, however, I learnt to pray for opportunities to talk about God in a natural way during my input and to do this with grace and sensitivity. I did not want to offend anyone or abuse the privilege I had been given to speak at these meetings. Yet I wanted to honour God as best I could and share in a real and vulnerable way. As it turned out, this resulted in many worthwhile and sometimes moving conversations with people at my book table after such events.

But perhaps the biggest challenge to staying real in the course of my writing and speaking journey was that old pitfall of pride. While my books might not be bestsellers, it was wonderful at times to hear how my readers appreciated what I had written and even how much a particular book had ministered to them. Also, after speaking somewhere, I would often receive encouraging comments about my input. I sensed it was right and good to receive these with grace and allow them to feed my spirit in a wholesome way. I could still remain humble while doing so, remembering how God had enabled me. Yet was I perhaps still seeking to boost my sense of self-worth through it all? Was I looking to others to affirm me rather than allowing God to tell me who I was?

I did not want it all to become a mere ego trip. I was well aware of the crippling self-doubt many creative people, including me, seem to have. But I had also noticed how some would veer towards the other end of the spectrum, exhibiting almost rampant narcissism at times. In between these two extremes, as I once saw portrayed in a diagram about artists and their personalities, was a small window where these two responses were held in perfect balance. I wanted to stay in that small window, listening to what God said about me rather than taking too much notice of others' opinions—or of my own opinion about myself. I wanted to stay real and humble, sharing from my true self and bringing glory to God. And, above all, I wanted to stay focussed on God, in the midst of pressures from without and within to do otherwise, and to resist the enemy, who delights in causing us to be less than the person God has called us to be. As David Benner states:

God's will for us is that we live out the harmonious expression of our gifts, temperament, passions and vocation in truthful dependence on God. Nothing less than this is worthy of being called our true self. Nothing less than this will lead to our deepest fulfilment. And nothing less than this will allow us to show the face of Christ to the world that we have been called from eternity to show.[31]

For reflection

- Is there some area of your life in which you find yourself often falling back into old, unhealthy and even childish ways of thinking? Take a moment to reflect on 1 Corinthians 13:11:

    When I was a child, I spoke and thought and reasoned as a child does. But when I grew up, I put away childish things. NLT

    Then, if you can, before God, name these childish patterns for what they are and ask God to help you put them aside for good.

- At this point in your life, where for you is that place '*where your deep gladness and the world's deep hunger meet*', as Frederick Buechner puts it?

- Is over-committing yourself an issue for you right now? Be still for a few moments, noticing how your body feels. Then ask God what you can do about this busyness in your life. What is it that you are missing out on most as a result? Continue to sit with God or a while and pray for a restoration of that balance you need, in order to function more out of your true self.

- What do you think about the concept of befriending ourselves? How do you feel this could tie in with the fact that God knows each of us inside out and loves us without reservation?

---

[31]   David Benner op cit p103-104

Chapter Thirteen

Coming Home

"Are you tired? Worn out? Burnt out on religion? Come to me. Get away with me and you'll recover your life. I'll show you how to take a real rest. Walk with me and work with me—watch how I do it. Learn the unforced rhythms of grace. I won't lay anything heavy or ill-fitting on you. Keep company with me and you'll learn to live freely and lightly.
Matthew 11:28-30 The Message

It seems a paradox at first that this journey home to our true self I believe is so important for us all to take is, in reality, a journey home to our Creator God. As Benner points out:

God precedes us on this journey, waiting to meet us in the depths of our self.[32]

At the same time, God is with us on this inward journey home, guiding us, drawing us on, wooing us in love. And, once there, we discover that finding our true self begins with experiencing new birth through Jesus Christ, as God re-creates us into that person we were meant to be all along.

... anyone who belongs to Christ has become a new person. The old life is gone, a new life has begun! 2 Corinthians 5:17 NLT

While this journey of coming home to our true self has deep inner

---

32   Ibid p 60

significance for each of us, it is also about living in this world each day out of that very centre of our being where God dwells with us. It involves a journey outward and onward, as we function out of the fullness of a soul transformed and being transformed by God. As God works in us, we find it is safe to remove those layers of our false self and to receive healing for those vulnerable parts of us that may have been bruised and damaged by the experiences of life. And, as we continue on that path of co-operating with God's Spirit, we find we are more and more able to function from that place of peace where our inner self and our outer self are no longer in such discord.

Some Christians are wary of such concepts as finding ourselves or discovering who we are or pursuing self-fulfilment in life. For them, these may seem far too self-centred and inward looking. And it is true that, unless God is the one to whom we look for meaning and purpose in life and in whom we find our home, we may well still be lost and fragmented at the end of our search—and even more self-focussed. Yet it seems to me that, as we come to know ourselves better and allow our renewed, God-shaped souls to shine through, we become more self*less* than self*ish*. Over time, as we function more out of that place of security and of peace with God, we learn to relax, knowing we are so loved and accepted. Like the precious, old toy in the child's storybook, *The Velveteen Rabbit*,[33] we become more real. We become less fettered, less inhibited, more transparent and more prepared to laugh at ourselves when necessary. We become less preoccupied with justifying or protecting ourselves and pretending to be other than we are. And we become more able to rejoice with others and to expend our energies helping them find themselves in God as well and become all they were created to be.

In short, as we allow God to remove those protective layers within us, the person who emerges is not so much we ourselves, but Jesus Christ as seen in us. Perhaps Eugene Peterson's rendition of Galatians

---

33   Margery Williams *The Velveteen Rabbit* Heinemann 1922

2:20 in *The Message* sums up this paradox best of all:

> *Indeed, I have been crucified with Christ. My ego is no longer central. It is no longer important that I appear righteous before you or have your good opinion, and I am no longer driven to impress God. Christ lives in me. The life you see me living is not "mine", but it is lived by faith in the Son of God, who loved me and gave himself for me. I am not going to go back on that.*

On one of my early trips to Turkey to see my friend, I experienced something I have never seen or heard anywhere else I have travelled. As the plane touched down in Istanbul, all the Turkish people on board around me cried out with joy and applauded. Now they were home. Now they were back in familiar territory. Soon they would be surrounded by the welcoming sights and sounds and smells of their homeland. Soon they would be able to relax in the company of family and friends who loved them and understood them. At times, I have experienced a somewhat similar joy, after returning home weary from a long trip. How wonderful it is to be greeted by someone who loves me, to be back in my own home, however small or old-fashioned it might be, to sit in that favourite armchair, to sleep in my own comfortable bed! At last, I am home. At last, I can truly relax.

This is how it is when we are at home with God. This is how it feels to know who we are at the very core of our being and to live our lives from that deep place where God keeps us company on a daily basis. Here at last, our souls are at peace, despite the battles that might be raging around us. And, from this place of deep security, we can venture out to fight those battles in God's strength and to live life to the full, with integrity of heart, clarity of purpose and true compassion for others.

Although I did not know it at the time, this sense of being at home with God and with myself was what I was longing for as I stood listening to that old hymn 'Oh that will be glory for me' at my school headmaster's funeral as a child. I am so thankful God kept seeking me out in the years that followed and called me in a way I could not resist. I will always treasure that special night at the camp when, as a fifteen year old, I realised for the first time how much I mattered to God. I can still remember how, in that instant, my basic reason for being here on this earth became so clear to me. And I am so grateful God continued to beckon me out from under those protective layers of mine and strengthen me to step out more and more to be the person God created me to be.

The Spanish Carmelite nun and mystic, Teresa of Avila, in her famous volume, *The Interior Castle*, written in 1577, says the following about knowing ourselves:

> *It is no small pity, and should cause us no little shame, that, through our own fault, we do not understand ourselves, or know who we are. Would it not be a sign of great ignorance, my daughters, if a person were asked who he was, and could not say, and had no idea who his father or his mother was, or from what he came? Though that is great stupidity, our own is incomparably greater if we make no attempt to discover what we are, and only know that we are living in these bodies, and have a vague idea, because we have heard it and because our Faith tells us, that we possess souls.*[34]

Why is it we so often miss those opportunities God gives us along the way to search our souls, to understand ourselves better and to find out who we are deep down? Sometimes we fail to see them at all—we are too busy focussing on other important things in our lives. Sometimes we may be too afraid to grasp them and to be honest with ourselves and with God. Instead, we choose to hide under those protective layers and to cling to our pretences, resisting any change or growth. And, in the midst of it all, the enemy delights to manipulate the fear and darkness in us and to prevent us from living our lives to the full in the way we are called to live as children of God.

At different times over the years, I believe I fell into these traps. In

---

34 Teresa of Avila *The Interior Castle* Christian Classics 2007 (originally published 1588) p 41

my late teens and early twenties, I thought, in my naivety, that I had it all together. As a young mum, I was too busy and preoccupied to realise how little I understood myself and my responses to the pressures of life. As a mature age student, I was too intent on showing I could still do everything well and on proving others wrong. In the workforce as a teacher and in other roles, I was too tired and stressed to think about anything apart from work and family and surviving week to week. In local church ministry, I was often too focussed on serving others and on trying to find my place in our team to care much at all about myself. At that point, and on into my writing years, I finally found myself able to look deep inside and to learn to be true to that person within who had been created by God for a purpose. Even then, I was fearful at times of exploring my inner world any further. Yet, through it all, I knew God was with me and would never let me go.

I can therefore well understand the reasons some of us might not choose to explore more of who we are until later in life. I have been there myself and, no doubt, am still blind to many things within me that need to change. Having said that, it troubles me when I see those who seem to have experienced that wonderful, new birth through faith in Jesus Christ, yet have not gone on to maturity as a believer or as a person. They may not realise it, but they are of little use as they are—and, in fact, can sometimes cause great destruction in the body of Christ. When we are immature in our responses to those around us, when we are jealous or threatened by others, when we are unable to honour others above ourselves, when we fight over this or that, when we withdraw as a way of protecting ourselves, God is dishonoured—and the enemy cheers. I have known church leaders who have left ministry because of the difficulties encountered in trying to lead immature believers. I have known believers who have left churches because of immature responses by leaders to issues in the life of the Body. I have seen many turn away from their faith altogether because of such situations. And I have heard and read much maligning of God and the church from those outside looking in who do not like what they see.

We are each responsible for our own lives and for our responses to the challenges we encounter. What a shame it is when we choose to remain children in our own inner life and in the way we relate to others, rather than become the person God is calling us to be! What a shame it is when we choose to hide from God and from others, rather than walk in the full freedom and fulfilment our loving Lord has for us! How much better it would be if we were all to put away those childish behaviours we cling to and instead move on with God, who knows us through and through anyway and watches over us with a fierce and protective love.

It is true we will not see everything clearly until we meet with God face to face. But it is up to us all to seek to understand as much as we can now about God and about ourselves and to grow into mature people and mature believers who in turn can help others grow. Throughout our lives, we are called to cooperate with the Holy Spirit in that remoulding process that can happen within us as we continue to walk with God. And that requires action on our part—the action of getting rid of the old, false self and allowing the new, true self to emerge that is being renewed day by day, as Paul explains to the Colossian believers:

Do not lie to each other, since you have taken off your old self with its practices and have put on the new self, which is being renewed in knowledge in the image of its Creator. Colossians 3:9-10

God's purpose for each of us is to reflect more and more of the image and nature of our Creator. In Genesis 1:27, we are told:

So God created human beings in his own image. In the image of God he created them; male and female he created them. NLT

This concept of being created in the image of God is difficult for our finite minds to comprehend, but what it means, in part at least, is that we as human beings are able to relate to God in a unique way. There is something about us that connects with God and something we have in common with God, although we are not God. But it also surely means that, as we relate to God, we are capable of reflecting something of what God is like to the world around us.

When a child reminds us of one of its parents in some way, we often say 'Oh, he's the spitting image of his father!' or 'Oh, she looks just like her mother when she does that!' We accept this as natural that a child might inherit some characteristics from its parents or share some of their mannerisms. In the same way, the fact that we are created in the image and likeness of God must mean we each possess something at least of the characteristics of our Creator. Yes, that image became marred and distorted once we chose to disobey God and go our own way, just as a wavy mirror at a fun park or an old, speckled one might give us a warped, inferior view of ourselves. But, through Jesus Christ, our capacity to relate to God has been restored. And, through the transforming work of God's Spirit within us who believe, that image of God will become visible again as we draw closer to God, learning how we are to live and respond to the world around us.

There is no doubt the enemy would prefer us to hold onto that marred and distorted image and forget about the high calling we have as human beings to reflect God to the world and to bring honour to our Creator. As Emily Freeman comments:

I can't imagine anything more dangerous to the enemy of our hearts than people who know who they are.[35]

How much more often could we spoil the enemy's plans, if we lived in intimacy with God each day, knowing who we are because we are grounded in God and reflecting the best image we can of God to those around us in the unique way we were created to do?

I like to think I am a passionate, committed speaker. Whenever I am invited to speak somewhere, I always ask God to bless and

---

35 Emily Freeman *A Million Little Ways* Revell 2013 p 15

encourage everyone present in some way. I also have a small prayer team of wonderful women who have agreed to pray for me wherever I go. Because of this, I believe God is with me every time I stand up to address an audience—and this gives me passion and confidence, as I endeavour to share from the depths of my heart. Sometimes, it feels as if a part of me is going out along with my words, as I give myself to connecting with those present, hoping to inspire them to reach out to God, to receive God's love, to forgive, to be the person God has created them to be. As a result, I have received some interesting feedback at times.

'Thank you so much for sharing from your heart with us today,' a young girl at a church event told me once, with tears in her eyes. 'I love the way your face just shines as you share your story.'

'You're very passionate in the way you speak and in all you do, Jo-Anne—I love your enthusiasm,' one lady at a community group commented. 'I can see you derive a lot of joy from your writing and speaking.'

At first I was taken aback by such statements. Should I perhaps tone things down a little? Should I be more restrained and reveal less about myself when I speak? Now, however, I have come to believe, through discussing this with family and friends, that being myself is the best way I can reflect the image of God in me to my audience and that the passion and warmth I try to convey is God's own love and compassion, reaching out to touch others and to make a difference in their lives.

I hope this is so. If it is, then that is the greatest compliment anyone could pay me.

How wonderful it is to watch those whose faces radiate delight when performing some service for others or when creating some work of art! To me, this is a sign they are truly embracing the gifts and abilities God has given them. They know who they are and what they can do. They are functioning from a heart grounded in God. And their heart's desire is to share something of their God with others, to be that face of God to the world they were created to be. I have observed the joy on the face of a friend based overseas, as she talked about the love of God with a group of women in her home, then prayed for them in their own heart language. Not long ago, I heard how a young man was able to use his business knowledge to make a difference in a needy country and how the joy and inner fulfilment he experienced as a result was so obvious to his family back home, as they interacted with him via Skype video calls. And I remember even now the speaker's shining face on the night I committed my life to Christ as a teenager, as he spoke with such passion and conviction. Each of these people had come home to God—and to themselves. And the joy each of them radiated as a result could not be contained.

If I had been told as a young girl that I would one day marry a minister, I would never have believed it. But it happened.

If I had been told as a young mum in South Australia that one day I would return to high school teaching, I would have laughed in disbelief. But it happened.

If I had been told during my second stint as a high school teacher that I would soon become an assistant editor, I would have said, 'I couldn't do that!' But it happened.

If I had been told in those editing years that my next move would be to a secretarial role in our church office, I would have been more than a little amused at the idea. But it happened.

If I had been told during those years of office work that I would end up at theological college and become part of our church's ministry team, I would have found it too incredible even to contemplate—just as I did when God spoke to me during my retreat. But it happened.

If I had been told in those ministry years that one day I would have eight books published, I would have said without hesitation, 'That's impossible!' But it happened.

When we journey with God, anything is possible. I love how

Eugene Peterson expresses Ephesians 3:20 in *The Message*:

> *God can do anything, you know—far more than you could ever imagine or guess or request in your wildest dreams! He does it not by pushing us around but by working within us, his Spirit deeply and gently within us.*

God is well aware of our situations and of everything that lies ahead for us. God knows when we feel overwhelmed with the challenges we face or believe we will face in the future. And God's desire, as this verse highlights, is not to coerce us in any way but to work with us and walk with us through all those challenges, until we reach our home in heaven. All along the way, God is so patient with us. So many times in my life, I have refused to listen to that still, small voice and, instead, have chosen to plunge on ahead and follow my own path. Sometimes, God has had to pull me up short and speak in a way even I could not ignore, yet it has always been in love and with such gentleness and grace.

And God is still calling each of us, with that same gentleness and grace, to listen—and to follow.

...

I leave my desk now, go to our china cabinet and take out my precious set of Russian dolls. With great care, I lift off each layer, just as God has done and is doing for me. I uncover that final doll and note how tiny she is. I cradle her in my hand and admire the work that has gone into making her. I note how she has been carved and decorated with such care. I know she is only a tiny, wooden doll, but somehow I see in her that precious kernel of my true self, created in the image of God.

I remember then how, for many years, I could not find this last, precious doll. Once, in showing the dolls to our granddaughter, I dropped this tiniest one and, being so small and light, she bounced and rolled out of sight somewhere. Afterwards, I hunted in every nearby corner and mourned when I could not find her. I knew she could not be far away, yet she seemed to have disappeared for good.

Then, one day, long after I had given up hope of ever locating her, I moved our whole china cabinet away from the wall. And there in the dust beneath it, I found her. With great joy, I wiped her shiny surface clean and stood her with her family once again, in that place of honour on the top shelf of my china cabinet. In my imagination, she seemed a little shy at first to be on display, so vulnerable and exposed. There was nowhere to hide anymore—she had no choice but to stand as tall as she could and face the world, letting others admire the beauty and creativity of her tiny form.

It seemed such a significant thing for me to do back then, to complete my little family in that way. It was an action filled with memories of the day I bought those dolls in London with my friend, but also with memories of how I as a real person had changed and grown so much in those intervening years. And it seems such a significant thing for me to do now, as I pick up this tiny doll yet again with loving care and stand her beside the others. She is so little and fragile. She wobbles at first, but remains upright—and I breathe a sigh of relief. Now she stands before me with pride alongside the rest of her family, an integral part of the whole, yet perfect and complete in her own right.

Like my true self—that little girl inside so filled with self-doubt, so afraid of what people would think, yet longing to show her true colours to the world and to be accepted for who she was—my smallest doll seems to know what it is like to remain concealed under those layers of other personas, wanting but not wanting to be revealed. She knows what it is like to have been lost under that dust beneath the china cabinet, neglected and almost forgotten, her beautiful colours and patterns hidden from the world. Yet now she stands erect, exposed for all to see. And, again like me, she seems content to have found her true place in the scheme of things. After all, it was what she was created to do—to be a vital part of this little family of wooden dolls who are incomplete without her.

As I gaze at her, I am filled with thankfulness that God has removed so many layers in my life and enabled me to be the person I was created to be. That insecure little girl inside me has grown and blossomed and gained so much more confidence, as she has learnt to rest in God's love. There have been a few moments when she has had difficulty standing straight and tall where God had placed her. There still are. There have also been moments when she chose once again to remain hidden beneath her layers rather than risk exposure, but they are becoming fewer as the years pass. And, by God's grace, that little girl and I have grown so much closer together that we are, I believe, now almost indistinguishable one from the other.

God has worked wonders in my life, remoulding me and enabling me to stand straight and tall in who I am. There is still more work to be done, but I know I am safe in the Master's hands. Our gracious God will never lose sight of me and will continue to transform me and strengthen me to be the person I was created to be.

At last, I am coming home. At last, I can be who I was meant to be for God.

And in the end, that is all that matters.

Please help me, Lord.
Enable me to find that sacred space
where I can meet with you.
Then you can gently take apart
the many layered Russian doll
that often seems to represent my life
and show me who the "real me" is,
so that I can embrace
all that I am, and all you have for me
with joy and thankfulness.[36]

---

36   Extract from 'Will the Real Me Please Stand?' taken from *It's Just You and Me, Lord* by Marion Stroud, published by Monarch Books. Text copyright ©2012 Marion Stroud. Used by permission of Lion Hudson plc.

For reflection

- Read the last sentence of Matthew 11:28-30 again from *The Message* as quoted at the beginning of this chapter. How 'freely and lightly' do you feel you are living right now? Are you enjoying keeping company with God?

- Do you think it is possible to live in all the fullness of being God's child and our true self at one and the same time? Why? Why not?

- Take time to read again the final stanza of 'Will the Real Me Please Stand?' by Marion Stroud. Sit with God in quietness, reflecting on where you are at on your own journey home to God and to yourself. Then, if you feel right about doing so, make this prayer your own.

- Perhaps you might like to create your own unique prayer of joy and thankfulness to God for your journey thus far of discovering who you are and who God is. Look back through the years and see the faithfulness and grace of God in all the events of your life. Ask the Holy Spirit to bring to mind those times when God rescued you or surprised you or overwhelmed you with loving-kindness. Then let those words of thanks flow from the depths of your heart to bless the Lord, either in written or spoken form. And may the Lord bless you in a profound way as you do.

www.ingramcontent.com/pod-product-compliance
Lightning Source LLC
Chambersburg PA
CBHW050537300426
44113CB00012B/2139